I0104963

A Reason to Unite

Hurricane Katrina and the Millions More Movement

The Honorable Minister Louis Farrakhan

Copyright © 2022 Final Call Foundation, LLC

All rights reserved.

ISBN: 979-8-9859218-4-7

Published by
The Final Call Foundation
under the auspices of the
Honorable Minister Louis Farrakhan

Editor's note:
This book is a compilation of articles of edited excerpts of addresses delivered by the Honorable Minister Louis Farrakhan that appeared in The Final Call newspaper.

CONTENTS

SECTION 1
The Birth of a Movement

SECTION 2
Hurricane Katrina: The Centerpiece of the Movement

An Appeal to All Those
Who Would Be a Part of
The Millions More Movement

For years, decades and centuries, leaders have arisen among us who have fought, bled, and died to see us united as a people. Willie Lynch, the Caribbean plantation owner, developed a set of protocols that would ensure, if followed, that Black people wherever we were found on the planet would never be able to unite. So, these seeds of dissention and division have worked 100 percent to keep the former colonial and slave-master's children in power over us. All that Willie Lynch advocated in 1712 continues until this very day.

Those who wish to maintain power and control over us are fearful of anything or anyone who might bring unity to a fragmented people, so every leader who showed such ability or skill was castigated, evil spoken of, falsely accused, imprisoned, beaten or killed, only for us to later learn how valuable they were, male and female, to our advancement as a people.

From the time that I was a little boy, I hungered to see us as a united people, and when I heard the voice of the Honorable Elijah Muhammad and Malcolm X, I believed that of our people.

However, in our lack of understanding of the universal nature of His Message, we were not permitted with our limited understanding to unite the whole of our people, but we were successful in uniting a segment of our people to produce the Nation of Islam as an example of what a united people could produce in the way of providing for our necessities of life.

The Honorable Elijah Muhammad called for a united front of Black leaders and organizations to plan the uplift of all of our fallen people. Kwame Ture, also known as Stokely Carmichael, carried the theme of a United African Front and worked to produce this to the end of his days.

I am so thankful to Almighty Allah (God) for the words that he caused me to write and say that have become the basis for the call of the 10th Anniversary of the Million Man March and the creation of the Millions More Movement.

For the first time in our history, those of us of different ideologies, philosophies, methodologies, denominations, sects and religions, political and fraternal affiliations have come together to create the Millions More Movement. Each of us, who have agreed to work together for the benefit of the whole of our people, have said from our particular platforms based on our beliefs or understanding or the lack thereof, things or words that have offended members of our own people and have offended others, and our ideology, philosophy, religion and pronouncements may have hurt the ears and sentiments of others outside of our community.

Therefore, this has kept us working inside of our own circles with those who think as we think or believe as we believe. As a result, some of us would never appear on the same stage with one another, for fear of being hurt by association with those with whom we have serious disagreements.

The Millions More Movement is challenging all of us to rise above the things that have kept us divided in the past, by focusing us on the agenda of the Millions More Movement to see how all of us, with all of our varied differences, can come together and direct our energy, not at each other, but at the condition of the reality of the suffering of our people, that we might use all of our skills, gifts and talents to create a better world for our ourselves, our children, grandchildren and great grandchildren.

I cannot fault a Christian pastor for standing on his platform to preach what he believes, nor a Muslim, Buddhist, Hindu, or a member of any religious or political party. All of us must be true to what we earnestly believe. I cannot fault a gay or lesbian person who stands on their platform to preach what they believe of self and how the world should view them.

Although what we say on our platform may, in some way, be offensive to others, we must not allow painful utterances of the past or present based on sincere belief, or based on our ignorance, or based on our ideology or philosophy to cripple a movement that deserves and needs all of us—and, when I say all, I mean **all** of us. We must begin to work together to lift our people out of the miserable and wretched condition in which we find ourselves.

Let us remember in this process that not one of us is qualified to judge the other, for none of us fully understands the circumstances, conditions and realities of each other's lives that make us to think and act as we think. Therefore, Allah (God) alone is our judge.

It is written in the scripture, *"Judge not, that ye be not judged."* **(Matthew 7:1)** Jesus again instructed us, *"How canst thou say to thy brother, let me pull out the mote that is in thine eye, when thou thyself beholdest not the beam that is in thine own eye? Thou hypocrite, cast out first the beam out of thine own eye, and then shalt thou see clearly to pull out the mote that is thy brother's eye."* **(Luke 6:42)**

These principles, if followed, will allow us to come into a common room with a purpose bigger than self and, in the process, create lawful dialogue to help us understand each other, that we may be shaped and molded, or reshaped and remolded, by our association with each other. The Millions More Movement, in causing all of us to be together for a common cause, allows the process of **lawful dialogue** to begin to help us in our exchange with one another in the best way. The Civil Rights Advocates, Nationalists, Pan-Africanists, Christians of every denomination, Muslims of every sect, students of every fraternity, Masons, Shriners, Elks to come into the same room and begin the process of lawful dialogue.

By our being able to exchange with one another in the best, most peaceful, and loving manner, we can help to shape and reshape each other's thinking. We are allowed to challenge each other's thinking if we disagree with each other in the spirit of love, and based upon truth and rational thinking, come to an equitable agreement. When we do this, we can begin to make ourselves into a mighty and powerful force for change.

Unity, love of self and love for one another have always been my desire. We stand on the threshold of the realization of our potential unity and the potential power that our unity can unleash to bring about a positive change today because of the Millions More Movement.

I am hoping that each of us will rise above our personal pain, hurt, or anger at one another for what we have said or done in the past or present to offend each other, that we might strive for reconciliation, understanding and agreement. Our very lives and the future of our people depend upon this; and this is why we say, "Long Live the Spirit of the Million Man March."

Let that spirit be the spirit of the Millions More Movement, and together we will achieve for our people and others in 10 years what we have not been able to achieve in the 450 years of our sojourn in this hemisphere.

It is written in the scriptures of the Bible, *"Not by might, nor by power, but by My Spirit saith the Lord."* **(Zachariah 4:6)** It is written in the Holy Qur'an: *"And hold fast by the covenant of Allah (God) altogether and be not disunited.*

And remember Allah's (God's) favour to you when you were enemies, then He united your hearts so by His favour you became brethren. And you were on the brink of a pit of fire, then He saved you from it. Thus Allah (God) makes clear to you His messages that you may be guided." **(Surah 3, verse 102)**

Thank you all for reading and striving to adhere to these words.

Signed

The Honorable Minister Louis Farrakhan

Amazing Grace:
Traveling to Sound the Trumpet

The firmness of the footsteps of the Honorable Minister Louis Farrakhan over the course of the 50 years in which he has served Black people through representing the Teachings of the Most Honorable Elijah Muhammad has proven not only his commitment to his teacher, but also his love for his mission and people. In trying to teach his humble student of his value to him, the Most Honorable Elijah Muhammad one day told Minister Farrakhan that he was more valuable to him than all of the diamonds and gold in the earth because, "through you, I will get all of my people." Minister Farrakhan's history of crisscrossing the 50 states of America on national tours can rival Joshua's circling of Jericho until the walls came tumbling down.

Certainly, his recent national tour mobilizing masses throughout the country to organize around the issues of the Millions More Movement makes clear that the full objective of his life is sacrificing the comfort of his own life in order to deliver a gentle word that can save and heal the lives of others.

With breathtaking speed and amazing grace, Minister Farrakhan completed a 23-city national tour, stopping in an additional four cities for private meetings and a four-city fact-finding mission on the devastation of Hurricane Katrina. Embarking his tour on August 14 in Milwaukee, Wis., he would ultimately travel to 31 cities within 44 days.

A righteous appeal

"The person whom God shall give you, give him your support and let him go his length, and behold in him the salvation of your God. God will indeed deliver you through him from your deplorable and wretched condition ... I charge you this day before my God to lay no obstacle in his way but let him go."

Written by David Walker in his famous "Appeal to the Coloured Citizens of the World" in 1830, these words capture the spirit surrounding the release of the appeal letter that Minister Farrakhan issued at the start of his national tour, to all those who would be a part of the Millions More Movement.

Although the naysayers, critics and slanderers are poised at every turn of the path of Minister Farrakhan, he is not a vain leader or an envious man; for it is his humility that allows him to overcome the evil that is spoken of his character and the stones that are thrown for his good works—he is not focused on himself, but rather on the rise of his people and all of humanity from the depths of darkness of this world.

Proving true the Biblical verse, "To one who is hungry, bitter is sweet," he offered a message that ranged from an unnerving wake-up call, a dutiful admonition, a loving chiding to joyful personal testimony, inspiring encouragement, and wise instruction. In every city that he traveled, they came in droves to see and hear him, packing in 1,200- to 2,000-capacity venues in most cities where rallies were held.

Some of the larger cities filled capacity crowds of 3,000 to 7,000 people in modern convention centers or beautiful landmark churches. He personally spoke to an estimated 60,000 people during his national tour. His reach extended to millions where he was able to deliver his message via radio, television, or the Internet via video and audio casts.

During the first leg of his tour through the Central region, the core of his teachings was the perpetuation of the protocols of division set forth by plantation owner Willie Lynch in 1712. He also detailed how the water, food and air are intentionally poisoned, cutting short the span and health of our lives, as well as the outsourcing of jobs, which cuts the economic lifelines of our communities.

"Where is your future, Black man and woman?" he asked repeatedly, stressing that Black people have become useless to this society, and therefore must be destroyed.

As he reached the East Coast to relaxed homecomings in Boston and New York, he settled into a rhythm, swiftly outlining Willie Lynch's Letter and how its application has kept us in a wretched, disunited condition through distrust, envy, and fear.

"It's time to lynch Willie!" he declared to several venues.

The Trumpet Blows The Final Call

He entered the Mid-Atlantic region as Hurricane Katrina hit the Gulf area, with an equal velocity and explosiveness. Filled with pain over the suffering of our people and our lack of unity, he roared, warning in the leadership meeting hosted by the Baltimore local organizing committee: "You should be careful when the Lamb of God turns into a lion."

Passing through Virginia, where the seat of the Confederacy in Richmond is worshipped to this day, and heading deep into the bowels of the country where southern trees bore strange fruit, the message of Minister Farrakhan transformed into a caution delivered in calmer tones.

As the tragedy of the botched relief efforts unfolded, Minister Farrakhan called for people to open their homes and hearts to care for those in need and neglect from the government. He shared for the first time during a press conference in Richmond, Va., that the Hurricane Katrina catastrophe highlighted the necessity for the creation of ministries that would serve the needs of our people in the face of failing government institutions.

The warmth of his memories going to college in North Carolina reflected in the hospitality of the Carolina venues unmatched in previous cities, such as a LOC meeting held as a luncheon in Greensboro or the high-spirited rallies in Charlotte and Columbia.

A certain joy filled his addresses in Atlanta, where Christian ministers who were not afraid to stand and walk with him, some offering bold statements and actions of solidarity. The last leg of his tour of the Southwest again centered on the survivors of Hurricane Katrina, who have become the focal point of organizing and mobilizing within the Millions More Movement.

"If reparations is our main focus, then these Brothers and Sisters, and the horror that they have been through, have to be healed," Minister Farrakhan said during a Sept. 27 town hall meeting the day after returning home from his tour.

"They have given us a reason to live, organize and maximize our power," he insisted. "We will be worthy of death if we do not rise in this hour," he warned, in a precursor to his subject for the 10th Anniversary of the Million Man March, "The Judgement of Allah (God) has entered America."

Dora Muhammad

Editor

The Final Call newspaper, 2005

1

By The Time,

Surely Man Is In Loss

This is a time for all of us to consider the Time. In the Holy Qur'an, there is a short Surah, or Chapter, called Al-Asr, "The Time." In the life of a Muslim, Asr is the time when the sun is midway between its zenith and its setting. It is in the afternoon, during which we perform Salat ur-Asr, or afternoon prayer.

This chapter reads: "In The Name of Allah, The Beneficent, The Merciful. By the time, surely man is in loss except those who enjoin one another to truth and enjoin one another to patience." As Muslims, all times of prayer are important to us, but Asr is very important because it is not only the time of prayer, but it is also the time of the setting of the sun on a particular world.

We are in the time of the setting of the sun on the present world and its rulers because this world and its rulers have ruled contrary to the law and will of Almighty God, Allah. So even though Allah (God) permitted the present rulers a season, He set a time for the demise of their world.

Both the Holy Qur'an and the Bible tell of prophecies of an hour when the Chastisement of Allah (God) on the people would be severe. In the Holy Qur'an, it reads: "The shock of the Hour is a grievous thing. The day you see it, every woman giving suck will forget her suckling and every pregnant one will lay down her burden. And you will see children grey-headed, and you will see men as though they were drunken, but they will not be drunk, but the Chastisement of Allah will be severe." The recent tsunami that we have witnessed in the Indian Ocean started with an earthquake, where the tectonic plates at the floor of the ocean moved, which created a vibration that set off the earthquake, which set off the tsunami and tidal waves that affected 11 countries. "By the time, surely man is in loss." Allah (God) is saying that there is a time—now.

The Bible says it differently: "For everything that is done under the sun, there is a time and a season and a purpose. There is a time to be born. There is a time to die. There is a time to sow and there is a time to reap. There is a time to gather stones and there is a time to cast stones away. There is a time to heal and there is a time to kill."

What time is it because, by the time, surely man is in loss; and the only way that you can lose is if you are not in accord with the dictates of the time. The sun is setting on the world in which we live. Those of us who are in love with this world, the sun is setting on you. The only way we can escape the destruction that is coming to the world is to get out of the way of what the time is dictating is about to happen: the Shock of the Hour.

The Honorable Elijah Muhammad said, "An hour has 60 minutes, and a minute has 60 seconds." The Book of Revelation says, "Count the number of the beast, for it is the number of a man, six hundred, three score and six." So, the Shock of the Hour is the time of the end of the present world and its system of things. It is so interesting that this quake started at the bottom of the ocean. "What is significant about that?" you may ask. It is significant because poor people are at the bottom of the world that the rich bloodsuckers of the poor have built on the backs of poor people. Nobody thinks about the poor. They only pay lip service to the poor. Who speaks for the poor?

Prophet Muhammad (Peace be upon him) was speaking one day to a highly placed individual and a blind man from among the poor was tapping his way up to the Prophet. He could not see, but he heard the Prophet's voice, and he knew of this man's greatness. As he came toward the Prophet, he interrupted the Prophet who was speaking to a highly placed individual, and the Prophet frowned on the blind man and his interruption of him.

Then, Surah Al-Abasa, "He Frowned," was revealed. But it was not that the Prophet frowned; Allah (God) also frowned, because he said to the Prophet, "You are spending time with this rich man who will probably never believe, but the blind man who is tapping his way up to you to seek you, you frown on him."

That is the way of the world today. They frown on the poor man because he is perceived as an interruption of what is going on. Some of us have reached a place where we only like to speak to those who have and we care not for those who have not. But the Bible says that, when Jesus spoke, the rich did not like his speech, but the poor heard him gladly. That is what made Jesus dangerous. The rich did not like the message of Jesus because Jesus, in truth, was a revolutionary.

"How can you prove that, Brother?" By his words. He said, "I came that those who say they see may go into darkness and those who are in the dark may come into the light." That is the way the Earth is as it moves. We are in the Earth's shadow now, so we are in the darkness, but on the other side of the Earth is morning. But as sure as it is night, we will enter into the dawn of a brand new day, and those who are in the light now will be in darkness. When the tsunami hit Southeast Asia, people were frolicking on the beach, without a care in the world, enjoying the beauty of the Asian waters, the nice warm temperature, and the white sandy beach. Tourists traveled with their families from the cold in Europe and North America. They were not concerned about the time.

"Surely man is in loss, except those who believe and do good and enjoin one another to truth and enjoin one another to patience."

One person said he was standing on the beach, and they weren't paying attention, and when they looked up they could not find the water. The water had receded from the shore and then came back to the land with a force, sweeping away all of the people who were on the beach.

The animals knew what was happening and they retreated to high ground. But the people who came to party, their carnal minds did not allow them to tune in to what was really happening. It was reported that there were some villagers who could smell the tsunami in the air; they could put their ears to the ground and feel something happening, so they retreated to high ground. All of those villagers were saved, because they understood something about the time and what was happening at that time.

Jesus was feared because the Roman authorities had built their power on the backs of the poor and the moment a message would come to poor people and start poor people moving, it is like those tectonic plates at the bottom of the ocean. It creates an earthquake. That is why the Caucasians in the South in America were always looking for a leader who would come and "disturb their n---s." So, they listened carefully to what our leaders say and how the people react, because they know that, as long as the masses sleep in ignorance, they can continue to rule them. But when somebody speaks to the poor and the poor begin to move, cracks begin to show in the institutions that are built on their backs, and these institutions begin to cave in.

Today, there is motion among the masses and that motion is creating cracks in the spiritual wall of religion. Preachers cannot just say anything anymore, because there is something happening among the poor if you don't teach them properly. They will not listen. There is a crack in the educational wall, so the children, though they are hungry for knowledge, they throw the "food" back because they do not like what they are receiving in this Western educational system. There is a crack in the political, judicial, and social walls in this system of

8

things. The more the vibration picks up at the bottom of society, then the buildings begin to sway, and you start bringing down the walls.

In the Bible, there is a story of Joshua walking with the people around the walls of Jericho. When they circled the walls for the seventh time, they began to shout. The sound and the constant stomping of their feet around the wall produced vibration. They were not simply walking around; they were making a vibration that was shaking the foundation of a wall that has kept them out. So, when they shouted, the foundation was already shaking, so the walls came down.

Black man and woman, the walls of America, the walls of racism and injustice are coming down because this is the time. But surely man is in loss, except you understand what the time demands. What does the time demand of us? For 400 years, we have lain at the foot of our oppressors begging to be let into their system. That is against what the time dictates. The time is not for you to try to get into the house with which Allah (God) is angry. The time is here for you to come out of that house.

In the Bible, it is prophesied: "Abraham, your seed will be a stranger in a land that is not theirs and they shall serve them and they shall afflict them 400 years." The scripture says, "But after that time, I will come and I will judge that nation which they shall serve. And afterwards, they shall come out"—not go in— "they shall come out with great substance and go." The coming out is a motion, but then the going is also a movement towards something.

The Bible continues, "And they shall go to their fathers"—not to their slave masters—they shall "go to their fathers in peace." Not just go any way, but they will go in the state of peace, and they will be buried in a good old age. Let us examine this prophecy. The Honorable Elijah Muhammad said, "We are living in the time of the Judgment."

Some of our Muslim family says, "No, that is not correct." But I want to ask you to think with me. If you study the Holy Qur'an, you will notice that there are more references to Moses than to any other prophet. Why? Is he more significant than Prophet Muhammad? No. Then, why is he mentioned more?

It is because he lays a prophetic picture that Allah (God) wants us to study. Why would Allah (God) speak to us in the Qur'an of prophets Noah, Lot, Shuaib, Moses, David, Solomon, and Jesus? He speaks to us of those people who were sent a messenger but did not pay any attention to the warnings and guidance of their messenger. So, by the time, they rebelled, bringing their destruction, which was a judgment that Allah (God) delivered against the wicked.

The Honorable Elijah Muhammad said the judgments against America would be unusual rain, unusual snow, and unusual earthquakes. He referenced the Book of Job in the Bible and snow treasured in the north. He referenced the fierce cold and strong winds that were used in the ancient times to destroy the wicked. Snow fell recently on the West Coast, with drifts that were 10, 15 and 20 feet, and winds of 168 miles an hour. If it were a hurricane, it would be five, in terms of its ferocity. But the media is not reporting these occurrences; instead they keep the people focused on what is happening in Asia, while you are blind to what is happening right under your foot. But what happened in Asia is coming to your door.

"By the time, surely man is in loss." You can take it or let it alone, but America will not escape and neither will you. We cannot play with the judgment of Allah (God). You have been playing with God all of your life. This government has been worrying about terrorism. But ask the people in Asia and Africa who have been terrorized by the tsunami if they were in terror, even though al-Qaeda was not bothering them. It was Allah (God), the Lord of the Worlds bothering them.

***

The Bible and Holy Qur'an say, "And the worst is yet to come." So, what are you going to do? You cannot play your life away. God is after you. You have a rendezvous with destiny and He is angry with you because you have heard a lot and you know a lot, but you act on very little of what you know. You do not play with a message that comes for your deliverance, which is Mercy and Grace from Allah (God). To even teach, warn and guide you is Mercy from God. But when you reject Guidance, Warning and Mercy, then what is next?

The Honorable Elijah Muhammad said, "What you see afar, pay attention because it soon will be at your door." Whether you believe it or not, you are very precious in the sight of Allah (God). You. You do not think that much of yourself, but Allah (God) sees in you what He created in you that is good for the world. He has a purpose for your suffering, and He has a purpose for your life.

***

The waking up of the masses of the people will bring about revolution. I yearn to see us stop the killing of one another in our communities. I yearn to see us fulfill the destiny that Allah (God) has for us and I am willing to give my life to see that happen. You are more valuable than I am. You are a great people, but you are mired in ignorance.

The scripture says, "My people are destroyed for the lack of knowledge." You are not an evil people, you are only evil now by circumstance, but you really are a righteous people. If we could separate you from that which has made you what you presently are, Allah (God) says He can make you into what He created you to be. But you have to come out of the present order of things and start motion toward your Father.

***

That's why the 10th anniversary of the Million Man March is significant, not from the march standpoint, but it is time to mobilize Black people like we have never been mobilized before.

The Honorable Elijah Muhammad said, "Our unity is more powerful than a hydrogen or atomic bomb." Your enemy is frightened of weapons of mass destruction. Why not let's try unity? We have tried everything else. We have kneeled, waded, crawled, begged, and slept in. We have marched and boycotted, but we have not tried the unity of us as a people. The Honorable Elijah Muhammad said, "If you tried it, our unity would solve 95 percent of our problems."

America owes us. If we went to Washington and put a demand note on the White House, the government would just look at it. But I would rather place the demand note and let them do nothing, because then we would see that there is no hope in a benevolent White man in the White House. The hope is in Allah (God) and in us. Reparation is real. To repair us is a serious work that needs to be done, but White people do not have the means to repair us, and if they had the means, they do not have the will. The Bible does not say that Pharaoh had what it took to repair the Children of Israel.

The Bible says, "He had healing in his wings." Wings, in this reference, represent that which allows you to fly above and defy gravity. It is not physical wings; it is the wings of knowledge that allow you to rise above the reality of our lives. "He had healing in his wings." The knowledge that

God will reveal through a proper study and administering of Bible and Qur'an will heal every broken and wounded human being on this earth. And it starts with you. So, even if we demand something from the enemy, which we should do, the biggest demand we should put is on ourselves.

You have the power to make a change in your life. The Holy Qur'an teaches, "Allah will never change the condition of a people until they change within themselves." But you cannot change on your own. You can want to change, and I am sure that all of us want to be better than what we are.

Having the desire to change is the right beginning, but what is the instrument to bring about the change? We are standing on a planet that the Honorable Elijah Muhammad taught us is 196,940,000 square miles, with a weight of six sextillion tons, traveling at the speed of 1,037 1/3 miles per hour as it makes its revolution around the sun and its rotation on its axis. As it makes its revolution, it makes four dips, giving us our seasons—which is change. But what produces these changes in seasons?

It is the Earth responding to light. The light of the sun—traveling 186,000 miles per second, striking the Earth at its equator—causes the Earth to spin. As the Earth is spinning because it is in submission to the power of the light, it produces spring, summer, fall and winter.

We are a people that the Bible says, "walk in darkness, gross darkness the people." In the darkness, we can make no change, because darkness is death, and in death there is no time or light. But the moment light comes, then the Bible says, "the people that walked in darkness have seen a great light."

One of the names of the Holy Qur'an is *Al-Nur*—not a light, but "The Light." There is a man in the Bible called Jesus who said, "I am the light of the world." The Qur'an says of the Prophet that, "he is a light-giving sun." So, if the Light of God, Al-Nur, shines on you and you respond to the Light, then the Light will cause motion and start time for you.

"By the time, surely man is in loss except those who believe and do good, enjoin one another to truth and enjoin one another to patience."

Light is present now. Respond positively to the presence of Light and make up in your mind tonight, "I am going to make a change." The moment you make that decision, then Allah (God) says He will step in: "I'll never change the condition until they change within themselves." If you respond to the Light, you will change within yourself. Then, Allah (God) will help you and us fulfill our destiny.

2

How Beautiful It Is
When Brothers Can
Dwell In Unity Together

In The Name of Allah, The Beneficent, The Merciful. We give Him Praise and thanks for His Mercy and His Goodness to the members of the human family. That Mercy and that Goodness is most exemplified by Allah (God) sending into the world prophets and messengers. Whenever a people stray from the path of His Divine Favor, before He punishes, He always raises someone to raise, guide, warn and remind the people that they should return to a right path, that they may be successful.

As Muslims—and that only means one who believes in submitting his or her will entirely to the Will of God—we believe in all of the prophets no matter where they were sent on this earth. We know that all of the prophets came from one source. We believe in all of the scriptures that they brought, for there is nothing from Allah (God) but truth. So whenever He sends a prophet, He sends them bearing truth.

As Muslims, we believe in Moses and the Torah, or what is called the Old Testament. As Muslims, we believe in Jesus and the Gospel of the New Testament.

We could not really be a Muslim if we did not believe in Jesus. As Muslims, we believe in Muhammad, (Peace be upon him and upon them). We believe in the Holy Qur'an, the Book of scripture that Allah (God) revealed to Prophet Muhammad (PBUH).

I am a student of the Most Honorable Elijah Muhammad. I could never thank Allah (God) enough for His intervention in our affairs in the Person of Master Fard Muhammad, the Great Mahdi or Guided One, Who came among us and spent three years and approximately four months and raised from among us one upon whom He would place a weighty word and a weighty assignment. That assignment was, and is, to give life to a mentally dead nation and, through that nation of people, give life to a world that is considered spiritually and morally dead.

I thank Allah (God) for the Honorable Elijah Muhammad and all that he taught that I was blessed to hear, all that he taught that I was blessed to understand, all that he taught that I was blessed to try to carry into practice. I greet all of you, my dear Brothers and Sisters, with the greeting words of peace. We say it in the Arabic language, "As-Salaam Alaikum," but it means in English, "Peace be unto you."

I am honored beyond words for what I see happening inside Black America. Even though we are suffering greatly, and the masses of our people continue to slide further down, I am finding among preachers, leaders and organizational activists that Allah (God) has placed a common thread that is allowing us to find the common ground that will allow us to put aside petty differences. He is elevating our consciousness beyond denomination. He is elevating our consciousness beyond our own organizational thrust, philosophy, or ideology to see, by His Grace, the bigger picture.

The bigger picture is, and must be, what we can do collectively to solve the problems that have plagued us, as a people, for over four centuries. We have the best-educated Black people in the world living in North America. We earn from this economy reportedly $750 billion a year—three quarters of a trillion come through our hands. We are not poor, we are just poorly organized. We are not poor in terms of material strength, but we are poor in terms of the poverty of the mind and spirit.

For the first time that I can recall, I traveled on February 26. I never go anywhere prior to the Saviours' Day convention or on the day of that convention. For several years, Brother Tavis Smiley has asked me to be a part of the forum that he hosts during Black History Month, and I have turned him down because of its closeness to Saviours' Day.

But last year, as I sat watching the forum on television, tears formed in my eyes, looking at Black scholarship, knowing how brilliant our people are, and knowing that the only thing missing is the unity of us, as a people. We have allowed our enemies to interpret us to each other. We have allowed the media to shape how we look at one another and how we feel toward one another.

***

There is no doubt in my mind that the power structure of this world needs to be upset. The hypocrisy of the rulers of this world needs to be exposed. The deceitful hypocrites who use good words to draw ignorant people into their web need to have their system exposed and their cunning made known.

When you have that kind of an assignment, everybody is not going to like you. When you have that kind of a mission, if you are not prepared to live and die for your mission, then you should leave the mission alone. We live in a world of fake Jews. We live in a world of fake Christians. We live in a world of fake Muslims.

If the real Jew, the real Christian, and the real Muslim stood up, they would stand together because they would be standing on principles of righteousness, truth, and justice. But when false Muslims, false Christians and false Jews beset us, the people get deceived who want to find God. The people get waylaid who want to truly serve God. That is why Satan must take over the mosque, church, and synagogue; and Satan has already done it. The church is not the church of Jesus Christ. Jesus would disown many of us who claim to be his. The mosque has been taken over by Satan. So has the synagogue.

So, will the real Christian please stand up? Will the real Jew please stand up? Will the real Muslim please stand up? The world needs to see what Christ intended, what Prophet Muhammad intended, what Moses and the prophets that came to the Children of Israel intended, but not this charade in the name of righteous men.

***

Recently, I met with some very precious, spiritual men who are Christian. At my table was a Pentecostal, a great bishop, Bishop Larry Trotter, who said that he lives to break down the walls of denominationalism. At the final analysis, we said, if you are Baptist, Jesus never said in the Gospel, that he was a Baptist. Do not waste your time looking for it in the Bible, because it is not there.

I want to be what Jesus was. Don't you? If so, we should not let a denomination stifle our relationship with our Christian family. Christ cannot be divided. Jesus never said, "I am Catholic," "I am Pentecostal," "I am Methodist," "I am Episcopalian" or "I am a member of the Church of God in Christ." He does not have anything to do with the labels that have divided the body of Christ. He is not pleased that we would exalt denominations over the meaning of his life.

When I was in Mecca, I met with Islamic scholars and wrangled over theology with them for three days. They wanted to know if I was a Sunni, Shiite, Hannifee or Hanbilee. No, I am none of these. I want to be what Muhammad was. He did not ascribe to any of these labels. Muslims have imposed these labels on the prophet to divide the house of Islam.

But what was Jesus? What was Moses? What was Muhammad? If you do not want to go deep into the meaning of your scripture and study this, then you want to continue in false worship. Abraham did not say, "I am a Jew." The Holy

Qur'an says he was neither a Christian or a Jew, he was an upright man and he was not of the polytheists. Yet, Jesus and Moses paid honor to Abraham as the friend of God.

Don't you want to be what Abraham was? Don't you want to be what Jesus was, what Moses was, what Muhammad was? If all of these great men were on this stage today, not one of them would be at variance with the other.

***

The Kingdom of God is a kingdom based on righteousness, not compromise. We have to make a decision whether we want to be with Jesus, Moses, Muhammad and God. If we want to be with them, we can only be with them in that which they are with—they are with righteousness. Righteousness does not have labels.

My mother taught me that five plus two equals seven. Your mother may have taught you that four plus three equals seven. Someone else's mother may have taught that six plus one equals seven. Another mother may have taught that seven plus zero equals seven. When the children get together, they start arguing over what their mothers taught them, believing everyone else is wrong.

But it is not that your mother was wrong. She knew in part, so she spoke the part that she knew. If we understood the basis of arithmetic, we would unite all the mothers and children, because understanding breaks down the things that keep non-understanding people divided and arguing amongst themselves.

Moses, Jesus, and Mohammed would never be found arguing. Never. Their love for God is translated into their love for each other.

3

A Declaration for
A Covenant with God

I want to say thank you, first to Almighty God for such a beautiful, beautiful
I want to say thank you, first to Almighty God for such a beautiful, beautiful
expression. As I listened to my Sisters and Brothers, my heart was filled with joy,
expression. As I listened to my Sisters and Brothers, my heart was filled with joy,
because this unity is something that I have longed to see since I was a boy.

When I was a boy, I read the Crisis magazine, given to me by my mom, and
I learned from W.E.B. DuBois about the struggle of our people. When I read the
Afro American and the *Pittsburgh Courier* and read about the lynching of our
Brothers and Sisters in the South, I felt the victimization of segregation in the
North and the bitter hatred of those who attacked us because we were Black.
Growing up in a West Indian family, I heard the different accents of the different
islands, but I also saw and heard the division between those who were born in the
Caribbean, those who were born in the United States and those who were born in
Africa, and the enemy's propaganda that pitted us all against each other.

Growing up in the North, I heard the hatred of Northern Black people
against our Brothers and Sisters from the South. I saw the color line, not only

between Black and White, but light-skinned Black people being pitted against the darker skinned Brothers and Sisters.

Growing up in an Episcopalian church environment—a loving church environment that gave me a wonderful foundation—yet, I was pained by the hypocrisy of church life. I never found fault with Jesus; I found fault with the hypocrisy of those who claimed to represent the love of God and the love of Jesus yet demonstrated hatred daily to Black people.

I saw my friends, young men with promise, join the armed forces to die on foreign battlefields for a freedom that we could not enjoy in this country. I watched the hypocrisy and viciousness of Jim Crow. I went down South to study in college and had to drink water from a "Black" fountain and go to a restaurant and go around the back, near a nasty toilet to receive a burger.

I thought about the price that our fore parents paid to build this country that is called the United States of America. We fought and died in the Revolutionary War for freedom that we still do not have. We were used by the British in the Revolutionary War and we were used by the North and the South in the Civil War. We have been used by successive governments to fight and die overseas and leave our bodies on foreign shores, only to come back home to a reality of rejection, hatred, and pain.

And through all of this, I longed to see us united and free, instead of seeing us as entertainers, who could entertain White people at night but could not live in a neighborhood near where we gave them joy with our songs, dance, and music.

If it were not for the Black Church, we could not have survived. The mournful songs of our Brothers and Sisters in the Deep South; our feeling and tarrying for the Holy Ghost made us live one more day.

Listening to Louis Armstrong, Billy Holiday and other artists who gave of their souls, we could go one more day in a vicious America. After all that Black people have suffered, we still have a heart of compassion. After all that we have suffered, we do not have a vindictive spirit, wanting to do to others what was done to us. If anybody deserves to strap a bomb on themselves and give pain for the pain that we have suffered, it is Black people. But none of us would kill innocent life for political purposes.

So, for me to be here this morning with my wonderful, esteemed, and brilliant Brothers and Sisters. This is a moment that I lived for: a Reverend Jesse Louis Jackson and a Reverend Al Sharpton and a Maulana Karenga and a Conrad Worrill and a Julianne Malveaux and a Cora Masters Barry and a Mayor Marion Barry and Mother Dorothy Height—all in the same room.

We did not come here by ourselves. We were brought here by the suffering of our people. So, when I listened to my Brothers and Sisters, I rejoiced in my soul, because death is hard when you work all your life to see your people free and die seeing them in a worse condition. When Dorothy Height, who is in her 90's, could say today, "I have been in all the movements and I have seen the frustration after the joy of struggle. But now, I have hope because of a Millions More Movement that will be led by all of us."

We have a mission that is bigger than all of us. Our ancestors' suffering is on our shoulders. They died and brought us to this moment, that we might do something to make a difference, not only for our suffering people, because we are a universal people. You are the mother and father of humanity, but our children are in a terrible condition, because we have gone to sleep in spiritual and moral death. But when we awaken, we will call the whole world back to the worship of God and to the brotherhood of humanity.

The Millions More Movement. We can never repeat the Million Man March. That was and it is done. Those who live in the past are dead. Those who are guided by the past can make a good present and are ready to prepare the future. So, as I sat listening to my esteemed family, I knew that all is well now. The suffering masses of our people have yearned to see this. When my Brother, Rev.

Jackson says, "Keep hope alive," we have done more today to keep hope alive in our people, just by our being here in the spirit that we are in this morning. We concerned about Black people because we are really suffering.

As Dr. Malveaux said, we are under attack. Thank God for the attack because, once we think that we are out of the woods, we go to sleep. So, the attack is awakening us. What I heard this morning is an awakened consciousness. We, on this platform, are dying. Every day, every second, every minute is moving us closer to the grave, so we have to be concerned about the kind of people we going to be.

What kind of Nation are we going to leave behind for our children and our grandchildren? You cannot only think about your pain as a people. God has used the pain of slavery to prepare us to free the whole of humanity from its pain. Sister Erykah Badu spoke of her "tears of joy." I knew I could not hold back my own tears today, because when you have been looking for something all of your life, you cry tears of joy when you finally see it.

I have never seen myself as greater than my Brothers and Sisters. I always have seen them as greater than myself and that is what makes it so easy for me to serve. And greater than we is out there in the world, that is why we are calling for the brilliance of our people.

We did not come to America on slave ships to be slaves for your entire existence. We did not suffer those years in chattel slavery to be clowns and buffoons today. What we went through had a divine purpose; what White supremacy put us through had a divine purpose.

The slave master can only be what he is because of the way he thinks. Racism can only exist in our manifestation of inferiority, but when we manifest the excellence of God, we kill White supremacy, and we save the White supremacist. America, you have to die in the old mind in order to live in a new world. The new world is not about color supremacy. The New World is based on righteous conduct and principled life—and that is what has brought us together, across all of these different religious lines, because there is a higher calling now.

Because we are in a room and spoke like we did this morning, there are those who would be joyous, and will say, "At last, the 'nigras' have come together to use the benefit of the knowledge they received in colleges and universities and the great teachers that have come among us, to solve their own problems." That is a blessing to America.

But there are others who are threatened that we all are here together. So, one by one, they will come to pull us away from our unity. They will ask, "How could you be in a room with bigots?" We lived with you, White people. They will ask, "How could you be in a room with racists?" We have been in the room with you, White people, for 400 years. They will ask, "How could you be in a room with those who are divisive?"

When White people brought us here, we were not integrated. We were in the holes of ships. We did not live with them. They put us to live in inferior dwellings and we had inferior food and treatment. We could not even be buried in the same cemetery with them. So, do not accuse us of being divisive.

The Million Man March inspired the world. Some people were angry with me when I left the country after the Million Man March for my World Friendship Tours, and they said that I had squandered a wonderful opportunity.

But everywhere I went in the world, as God is my witness, the kings and rulers received me. In some countries, the people lined the streets from the airport to our hotel. They were not applauding only me; they were applauding us, as a people, because they saw in us hope—that if we were unified in this country, we could affect foreign policy that was killing them in Africa, the Caribbean and Central and South America, as well as in the Isles of the Pacific.

So, God has called us to this moment. By whatever name you call Him, we could not be in here together if He had not called us. He called us to serve His purpose, not only to free our people from their suffering, but we called it a "Millions More Movement."

Millions More. We already had millions at the Mall for the Million Man March. Our Sisters had millions in Philadelphia for the Million Women March. Our youth organizers in New York and Atlanta had hundreds of thousands for the Million Youth March and the Million Youth Movement. "What do you mean millions more?" you may ask.

Millions more means that we are reaching for the millions who carry the rich on their backs. Millions more means we intend to create a tsunami, because the tsunami in Asia started at the bottom of the ocean—and the rich live from the poor, but the poor have no advocates.

The Democratic Party has a donkey for a symbol and the Republican Party has an elephant for a symbol. But Jesus loved donkeys, too, in a way: The Master said to his disciples, "You will see an ass, with a colt tied with it. Untie them and if anybody asks you,"—in other words, we know that you are going to be questioned when you start untying the ass and the colt—tell them that the Master has need of them."

When you are tied up but not being utilized properly, that means somebody owns you who has abused the right of ownership. So, a new owner has come—and the new owner told the disciples, "Untie the donkey." And Jesus rode into Jerusalem on that donkey, while they were saying, "Hosanna! Hosanna!"

So, on October 14th, 15th, and 16th, we are going throughout the land untying the donkey and the young colt, because the Master has need of these Black, Hispanic, Native Americans and poor White folks. The Master has need of you. So be ready to be untied.

I would like to see us, on October 14, say to the world that we are setting a new standard and a new paradigm. I want the Muslim world to be affected by how men and women work together to solve problems. I want the Christian world to be affected, to stop misusing women and stop thinking that women cannot be true servants of God, like men. I want the Jewish world affected. I want the whole world affected by what we do.

We are not going to let the hatred of Arabs, Christians and Jews affect us. We are Black Christians, Black Muslims, Black Jews and we want you to come follow us, because we are at peace with one another and we hope to bring you to peace with each other.

4

Operational Unity and
Grassroots Organizing

Look at your beautiful body. It is the true house of God if you let Him in. Jesus said, "The Kingdom of heaven is within you." How? Your nature is from God. It is polluted now, but it just needs reform and cleansing. That is why the Bible says the first Adam was made from dust, but the second Adam is made of a quickening spirit. Once your spirit is quickened, the God within you starts rising up to condemn the evil of yourself.

The more I studied our nature, the more I understood operational unity. Our bodies started from sperm mixed with ovum, which then created one cell. That first cell of life then divided and multiplied. A clot was formed, then an embryo, a fetus, a baby, a child, then a mature man and woman. You started from one cell, but you are now billions of cells, all working for one common cause. This is operational unity.

The brain is the brain. You do not see any bragging in the body. "I am the brain. I am the boss here, so you all better do what I say." The brain is functioning, the kidney is functioning, the liver is functioning, the lungs are functioning, the stomach is functioning, the tongue, teeth, hard palate, soft palate—everything in the body is functioning, but yet there are differences. In the nine systems of the body there are differences and the organs do not resemble each other, but they are working together in operational unity.

Brother Conrad Worrill may wear dreadlocks. I choose to wear my hair short. I shave, but my Brother may have a beard. But am I better because I shave or is he better because he has dreadlocks? Why are we going to allow these things to interfere with operational unity? What is the goal of the body? It is to survive. The body is set up to overcome any impediments within and without. This is operational unity.

But what makes the unity of the body purposeful is a cause bigger than the heart, the lungs, the liver, the kidneys, the intestines, or the spleen. All of them have a function and an agenda, but the cause unites all systems for the common good of the whole.

For the first time in our history in America, on May 2, 2005, in Washington, D.C., the NAACP, Urban League, SCLC, the National Black United Front, integrationists, nationalists, Pan-Africanists, those who are pushing reparations, the mayor of the city, Christians, Muslims, Hebrews—all of us were on the same stage. We were not changing our organization or our religion, but a common cause has given us a common purpose that is bigger than our organizations, religious denominations, or affiliations.

That purpose is to save a people who are dying, while a few of us are living better. That is why the Million Man March was successful, because it overcame barriers that would keep us from each other. The barriers that keep us from each other are artificial and man-made; they are not real. You say you are a Christian. So am I. "I thought you said you were a Muslim," you may ask. Well, I am that, too.

"Well, I know you are anti-Semite." No, I am a Jew, too. Why would you allow labels to divide the people of God? The Books of Matthew, Mark, Luke, and John in the Bible contain some of the words of Jesus Christ. Show me in the

Gospels where Jesus said, "I am a Christian." It is not there. He said, "I am the way. I am the truth. I am the light. I am the good shepherd. I am the true vine, and my father is the husbandman. I am the door. I am the resurrection and the life." He is all of that, but he never said once, "I am a Christian." So why would you use the name given at Antioch by the enemies of Christ to divide the people of God.

Some Christians say, "I am Baptist," but Jesus never said that, though he was baptized by John. He said that was a water baptism, but that there was one coming after him that would baptize us with fire in the Holy Ghost. What is that?! Everything has its form, but when fire touches it, fire breaks its form down and it becomes ashes. Jesus said, "I am the light of the world." The light of the world is the sun. The Holy Qur'an calls Muhammad a light-giving sun. That means that the word of Jesus is like fire. He was baptized with water, but he represents fire. The scriptures say, "I was born in sin and shaped in iniquity."

That is the way you are. But when you meet the fire of the word of Jesus, that fire breaks down the form of wickedness and the shape of iniquity and takes you down to ashes and builds you back up as a righteous man and a righteous woman. That is the Jesus Christ that I know. That is the Muhammad that I know.

So, I am a Christian. It means one crystallized into oneness with God, following the example of Jesus Christ. I am trying to follow his example and that is why I am persecuted. If you are not being persecuted, you should examine who you are following. Jesus said, "You will be hated for my name's sake." So, if you are not hated, persecuted for his name sake, cast into prison and brought before the courts of this world, falsely, you do not know Jesus.

He was in ancient Rome; we are in a modern Rome. I want to illustrate to you how I am following Jesus. I am not just talking Jesus; I am living Jesus. Did the Roman authorities like Jesus? Do the modern Roman authorities like Farrakhan? Who were the scribes? "Scribe" comes from the Latin word *scribo*, which means "to write."

How do the writers write about me? How do the religious leaders think of me? Jesus went in the synagogue, but he did not stay there, because he knew it was filled with hypocrites. So, Jesus went into the highways and byways. He did not travel with a choir, although we are supposed to sing songs of praise. He did not have any musicians. The music was the Word. The choir was those who said "amen" and lived the Word.

When the choir of this church sang earlier, "He woke me up this morning and I'm on my way," I saw you in the audience moving to the rhythm. We are a groovy people, but you do not have the right rhythm. Jesus said, "I piped to you all the day long and you have not danced." There is a rhythm to truth and it has a groove. Truth is so magnificent. When you want to get in the rhythm of truth, you are on time with the beat of the Master, as he is on time with the beat of His Father. Jesus said to God, "Whatever you bid me say, that I say. Whatever you bid me do, that I do." Even though the rhythm of music is good, it is best for you to dance by the rhythm of the Word of God. He said, "I lamented to you, and you have not mourned."

Look at the condition of our people. Don't you think we ought to lament and mourn over what is happening to us? What is needed is grassroots organization and operational unity. In Kansas City, and every city, there must be a strong local organizing committee that is not only for the 10th Anniversary of the Million Man March, but for a movement!

Movement. Where are you going if there is a movement? The Bible explains it with beautiful parables. Naturally, when somebody gives you the command "go," the next question you want to ask is, "where?" That is movement.

Pharaoh had the Children of Israel in bondage. Moses told Pharaoh, "Let my people go." Look at the words: not "free" —let them "go." Go where? There was a land and Moses wanted to get his people away from Pharaoh. Jesus met Lazarus at the tomb, and he called him out of the tomb and he said, "Satan, loose him and let him go." In the 15th Chapter of Genesis, it reads: "Know of a surety Abraham, your seed is going to be a stranger in a land that is not theirs and they're going to serve them and they're going to afflict them 400 years. But after that time, I will come and I will judge that nation which they shall serve and afterwards shall they come out with great substance and go to their fathers in peace."

Jesus told a parable of the Prodigal Son, who left his father's house and tried to join on to be a citizen in a strange country, like Black people in this country who say, "I am an American. I was born here." Who said so? Brother Malcolm X said, "Cats can have kittens in an oven, but that does not make them biscuits."

If you do not have the rights, privileges, and guarantees of an American citizen, then you have to ask yourself, who you are fighting for, why are you fighting, and why are you dying? Are you really an American? "Come out of her my people, that you be not partakers of her sins and her plagues."

When the prodigal son fell down in that strange land, the Bible says that a famine arose and then he thought about his father's house. He said, "I think"—he started thinking—"I will rise." He was lying down before. He said: "I think I will rise and go to my father." He started moving toward his father.

The Bible ends with the Chapter of Revelation. Do you understand? You started with your Father, the Creator. You started with Africa. Now, you must arise and return. You do not have to go to Africa physically, but you must come out of the mind that your slave-master created for you, because the mind that you are in is self-destructive because he made you hate who you are.

This is the opening of the National Black United Front's annual convention. "Why are you here, since you are a Muslim?" you may ask me. I love my Brother and I love what this organization stands for. I know we are not going where we need to go until the Nation of Islam can lock arms with the National Black United Front, the NAACP, the Urban League, the Crips, the Bloods, the people in the street, church, mosque, and synagogue, with a common purpose and operational unity. Brother Conrad Worrill has never infringed on who I am and what I do. I have so much love and respect for him. I have never tried to infringe on what he is and what he does to further the cause of the liberation struggle of our people. This is not a cookie cutter struggle, where you make everybody in the image of your idea.

Operational unity demands that we respect each other, where we are and the common purpose is bigger than who we are. That common purpose is to save a people and prepare that people, literally, to be an instrument to save a world.

5

The Value of the Female

Why are women important? Why is women's participation important for the creation of a Millions More Movement? To go right to the heart of that, no movement is going anywhere without the woman.

I would like to share with you some of what I was taught by the Honorable Elijah Muhammad of the value of a woman. I am hoping that the word that God lays on my heart and mind to speak to you will resonate in your hearts and minds, that you will begin thinking on a higher level about who you are and how valuable a woman is in the sight of God.

The Honorable Elijah Muhammad said that the first act of creation after the Self-Creation of God, He studied Himself, knowing that it was painful and difficult. He studied Himself and brought from Himself a second self. The female, according to the Bible, is a part of the man. But she is more than a part of man, the woman is the second self of God. Sisters, if you know why you are as you are, it makes it better for you to be yourself.

You are not the woman of man; you are the woman of God. The more men grow to reflect God, then the hearts of women will calm down and you will be more at peace. You are not at peace today. You are very disappointed, disillusioned and hurt by us, because you expected something and did not get what you expected. An illusion attracted you, but reality woke you up. Were you wrong to expect? No. Why do you expect something from a man? The Holy Qur'an deals with the nature of things because no person can rule unless you understand the nature of that, which you are trying to rule. You must understand your own nature, in order to develop self-mastery.

What is the nature of the woman and what is the nature of the man? The Holy Qur'an says, "Men are the maintainers of women." It is the natural role of a man to work hard and produce what is necessary to maintain a woman and the children that are produced from that woman. As a maintainer, he is a protector, provider, and he is supposed to guide. You cannot guide a woman with sex, and if a man is dumb enough to think that sex can guide a female, then the marriage falls apart and the relationship tumbles down.

Guidance comes from the brain, not from any other part of the body. Guidance must manifest wisdom and since you are the second self of God, then the man must bring to you wisdom and truth that is from God, because the only thing that can maintain the woman of God is the word of God, rightly brought from a man who is in the image and the likeness of God.

When a man works hard to maintain support, guide, and protect his wife and family, what comes up out of his wife is a natural desire to console, comfort and give that man peace and quiet of mind. When you fall in love, it makes you want to serve. You do things to please, whether it be in a meal, the way you fix your home, or the way you fix yourself. You try to make it nice for him because he brought that out of you by being what he is supposed to be.

But when he acts the fool, he shuts you down and you do not have any desire to console, comfort, cook or clean for him. You don't even want to rear his children, especially if they look like him. Sisters, something has happened to us, as men, and something has happened to you, as women. Something terrible has happened to men because we can attract you, but we cannot hold you. We can give you children, but we do not know how to help you rear them. We can make money, but we are rather selfish. Women have been greatly misused and abused. It is so painful that we live in a world that has raised sex to the level where we get lost in a pleasure that was to create a heavenly existence. The more we get lost in it, the more painful our life becomes.

So, having raised sex to the degree that a Satanic mind has raised it, men have lost respect for the second self of God and the second self of self. Men, then, use women for pleasure and discard women as you would a wrapper from a cookie, cake, or candy. It was sweet to you, but you cannot use the wrapper, so you throw it away.

The worst part of this sexual madness is that fathers have sometimes abused their daughters; uncles have sometimes abused their nieces; grandfathers have abused their grandchildren; and cousins and brothers have abused their sisters. When a woman is innocent, a virgin, and is raised in a wholesome environment, she loves purely. The first love of a girl in a wholesome environment is the male image of her father. She wants to serve, and she loves to be hugged by her father because it gives her a sense of safety and security because, by nature, you desire to be made secure.

The man's nature is the same. He desires to be made secure. A woman is made secure in a good man and a good man is made secure in God. So you have a natural sequence, as the Bible teaches: God is the head of man, man is the head of woman, and woman is the head of a child. When this natural order functions properly, there is joy and peace.

***

The Honorable Elijah Muhammad said, "Civilization is measured by the woman." If you want to take the world down, the place of attack is the female. If you want to build a world up, you start with the female. One day, one of the companions of Prophet Muhammad asked, "After God and His Messenger, who should we honor next?" The Prophet said, "Your mother." He said, "Who after that?" Prophet Muhammad said, "Your mother." The companion asked again, "Who after that?" And Prophet Muhammad said again, "Your mother. Then next, your father."

A woman is three-times the value of a man, because she brings forth life. Women teach and train the offspring. So, if you are an ignorant, unlettered, and foolish woman, you will make a foolish people. So when somebody wants to take the world down, they destroy the value of knowledge in a woman.

How could the Taliban say that they are Muslims and deny education to a female? When you deny education to the female, you are denying it to a nation. When you deny education to a man, you have denied education to an individual. When you deny it to a woman, you have denied it to an entire people. That's how valuable a woman is. We have to recognize that something went wrong with us.

In *The Final Call* (Volume 24, Number 44), the infamous Willie Lynch letter is reprinted. Every one of you should study this letter because he wrote this letter in 1712, yet 300 years later, what he wrote and what he carried into practice still exists among the Black, Brown, Native Americans and, even now, you can see it reflected among Caucasians.

You are very independent as a woman and some women are quick to say, "I don't need a man for nothing!" And you are not lying. You go to work every day. You bring your money home. Some women are foolish enough to keep a man while he is making excuses for why he cannot work. She speaks to him as she speaks to her child, because she is taking care of him.

How did the roles get reversed? Willie Lynch, a White Caribbean plantation owner, said: "Both horse and niggers are no good to the economy in the wild or natural state. Both must be broken and tied together for orderly production, for an orderly future. Special and particular attention must be paid to the female and the youngest offspring. Both must be crossbred to produce a variety and division of labor. Both must be taught to respond to a peculiar new language, psychological and physical instruction of containment must be created for both.

"You can't sleep, because if they are left in their natural state, they might kill you in your sleep. They sleep while you are awake and are awake as you sleep. They are dangerous near the family house, and it requires too much labor to watch them away from the house. Above all, you cannot get them to work in this natural state. "Therefore, both the horse and the nigger must be broken, breaking them from one form of mental life to another. Keep the body and take the mind.

"You must keep your eye and thought on the female. Keep your focus on the female but concentrate on the future generations. Therefore, if you break the female mother, she will break the offspring in its early years of development and when the offspring is old enough to work, she will deliver it up to you, for her normal female protective tendencies will have been lost in the original breaking process." Here is how they did it.

They desired to reverse nature. Instead of the female being dependent on her natural male counterpart, the slave-master wanted to make you completely docile and dependent on him. He did not want any Black or Brown woman to depend on her man. When he reverses nature, a female is produced that will be independent of that male figure, but dependent on the slave-master, and a male will be produced that will be dependent. The female that you produce will be independent of the male image—just like women today.

Today, our girls are independent, while our boys are broken. Women have broken their male children, unknowingly, but this is the way the slave-master fixed you. Willie Lynch said, "Take the female and run a series of tests on her to see if she will submit to your desires willingly."

These are White people who know the nature of things, plotting the destruction of an entire people by taking the female down. He said, "Test her in every way because she is the most important person in the making of a slave."

Sisters, if you are the most important in the making of a slave, then you are the most important person in making a people free. That is why there can be no Millions More Movement without women playing a proper, equal, and even dominant role.

Willie Lynch wanted to destroy the male image in the woman's eyes completely, so she would not look at any man in her race with honor and respect. He said, take a strong nigger man and have that woman and her child watch. You take two strong Black men. The first one you tie his hands and legs to a horse on both sides, then set that nigger ablaze. As the fire touches the horses, they start running in opposite directions and pull the Black man apart. The woman is horrified and so is the child.

Then, you take the second strong nigger male, and you take a bullwhip. You do not kill him; you beat him until he is nearly dead, and you make her watch this. She will go into a frozen psychological state because the man that nature tells her to look to for maintenance and protection, she cannot get it from him because she saw a White man pull a Black man apart and beat another Black man within an inch of his life.

Then, Willie Lynch says, "Now, you have reversed the roles. For the fear of the young male's life, she will psychologically train him to be mentally weak and dependent, but physically strong." You have trained your boy children and men to be docile in order to live. You broke the man yourself. Your girls grow up psychologically independent, so the female trains her female offspring to be psychologically independent.

So, we have the nigger woman out front and the nigger man behind and scared. So when you get married, he seems like a man. He's handsome and has really attracted you, but he has already been broken. After you marry him, you realize he is weak and so you start looking somewhere else, only to find somebody else who is in the same state.

You run from one man to another, and you end up disappointed with this man, disappointed with the next man, and disappointed with the man after that—so why not stay with the man you have and help make him into a man?

It may be easier said than done, but Sisters, we have to break the cycle and the reversal of nature because it is the reversal of nature that keeps you very, very unhappy and disappointed as a woman. You are not a lesbian. You may have a woman who you are with, but you are not a lesbian. You are just so upset with men and so hurt by men that you would rather lay next to a woman who shares your pain. But the moment a real man comes along, you'll get up out of bed with that woman.

Every Black leader who has ever tried to reverse this process has been falsely accused, maligned, brought to jail, beaten, and even put to death. White people, in order to rule, must keep the process the way they made it so that you will always look to the Caucasian.

As a woman, your nature is to be made secure. If your husband works downtown and is bringing home money, you are very happy because you know the bills are going to get paid, and he will be able to get you the little things you need or want. But let him tell you, "Honey, I went to sleep last night, and an idea came to me for a business, and I think I'm going to leave corporate America and go into business for myself." His first opponent is right in the bed next to him. "You're going to leave your good paying job to go out on some foolish idea to go into business for yourself? Who do you think you are anyway?" You criticize him.

Your nature is to be made secure and you are not sure that he will be able to make you secure by going into business rather than staying on the White man's job. So, in the house, there is a tug of war between the male and the female.

***

God created a woman's form to be appealing to a man's eyes. You can call him holy, you can call him divine, you can call him prophet, you can call him saint, you can call him apostle, but if he is a man, your physical form is appealing to his eyes. The Holy Qur'an says you were created to give him peace and quiet of mind and to be a consoler for him, so every aspect of you reflects this. But that beauty of you is not for every man to see. The beauty of you is for that special individual who has earned the right to be consoled by what you offer. But Satan said no.

How were women dressed 60 years ago? They covered from the top all the way down. It was not considered proper to wash your underwear and put them on a line in your backyard so that your neighbor can see what your underwear looked like.

A Black man in the South would get killed simply for looking under a White woman's dress on a clothesline. If the enemy saw him, he would know that not only would he look under her dress on a clothesline, but he was angling to get under her dress in real life; so he would kill the Black man just for that.

Over the past 60-70 years, look at how women have been taken down; and when you go down, you take us down because the Honorable Elijah Muhammad said, "Where there are no decent women, there are no decent men, for the woman is the mother of civilization."

When World War II came, he took women out of the kitchen. Most of you today do not know how to cook, but you want to get married. When he put you in the factories, as the men went to war, women became the top breadwinners. As men came back from the war, society was changing, and they had a new style of clothing for the women.

Long dresses were out, and gradually the hemlines rose and he began taking your clothes off. In the Book of Revelations, there is a description of a beast, with a woman dressed in scarlet sitting on top of the beast, because the beast is going to use the woman to attract the man to his destruction.

Then gradually, your clothes start coming off and the dances and music began to change. Now that he has taken you down like this, your attracting power has nothing to do with the way you think. Your attracting power is your sex and your willingness to give yourself to a man. Music is now all about sex. In order to groove to a beat, the body is moving, but what you are doing is the sex act standing up. When you go to the disco or a party, what is in your mind?

We can tell what is in your mind by how much flesh you are showing. You may say, "This is just the style," but you are not creating any style. Satan is creating the style to take you further and further down, so that civilization now is in a degenerate state because the woman is in a degenerate state, and there are no holy men. We have been ruined and so have you. So, Sisters, the Millions More Movement is about repairing the damage that was done to us through slavery.

***

You can be disappointed with your man, but if you keep beating him down with your mouth, you will always be disappointed. In his nature, he knows he is supposed to be the boss even though he does not have what it takes to be the boss. But, Sisters, if you really want to have peace in your home, learn how to handle your man in his ignorance and foolishness, because when God said, "Let us make man," He needs your help. If you do not help God, you will not find a man that will satisfy your soul. We need your help. We need your support.

So, are you willing to be a part of the Millions More Movement? Do you want to reverse the condition in which the enemy has put us and go back to the natural way? If you do, then let's go to work.

6

Black America:

A Product of Willie Lynch

Whenever God gives a people Divine Revelation, with that Revelation is a ruling scepter, that He might lift that people from an ignominious state and raise them to eminence. You are not who you are without God and you have not suffered what we have suffered except that it was a part of the Divine plan of Almighty God.

You may ask yourselves the question, "Why would God allow a people to suffer the worst form of slavery that has been inflicted upon any people in the annals of history?" As a Christian people, you should ask yourself, "Why would God allow Jesus, who is called His son, to suffer what he suffered? What plan did God have in mind by the suffering of a servant that, by his stripes, all humanity could be healed?"

In the 9th Chapter of John, Jesus was walking with his disciples and he came upon a man who was born blind. The question was asked, "Who did sin that this man was born blind? Did his mother sin? Did his father sin? Did he sin?" Jesus answered, "Neither his mother nor his father nor did he sin, but he is born blind that the works of God might be made manifest in him."

Why are we in this condition out of which nobody can get us? So that the works of God might be made manifest in us. He did not choose us with silver and gold; He chose us out of the furnace of affliction.

I am deeply, deeply, deeply concerned about the condition of America and the condition of the Black, Brown and Red people and poor people in America. The poor people have no advocate. The poor are the base upon which the rich build their riches. The rich desire to keep the poor ignorant, so that they can continue to be rich at the expense of the poor. Anyone who will come to organize, mobilize, stimulate, motivate, and agitate the poor will be considered an enemy.

America is your "Calvary." Your hands have been nailed, so they do not defend or protect you, or build anything for your people. Your feet have been nailed, because you have been here longer than any other people but have less to show for it in terms of productivity for yourself and your people. So, you have not moved relatively.

You have been pierced in your side. They said they educated you, but it is like putting a crown of thorns on your head. Your education makes you feel that you should make progress, but you are still where you are. You come out of one school and go to another; you come out of one fraternity and go to another; you come out of one Lodge and go to another.

But everywhere you go, the crown of thorns make you say, "Something is wrong." Jesus cried, "Eli, Eli, lama sabachthani! My God, my God, why have You forsaken me?" And that is the cry of Black America: "God, what is wrong? Why have You forsaken me?"

God never forsaked Jesus and He never forsaked us, but we had to endure such suffering in order for God to give us the blessing that is written in the scriptures—that the last shall be first and the bottom rail will come to the top and thou shalt no more be the tail, thou shalt be the head. This is the Lord's doing and only the Lord can do it and it is marvelous in our sight.

"Our Father, which art in heaven, hallowed be Thy Name. Thy Kingdom come. Thy Will be done on earth..." If God's Will is going to be done on earth, how will President George Bush fail? Will he be able to stand up? Will President Hu Jintao of China be able to stand up? Will Chancellor Gerard Schroeder of Germany or President Jacques Chirac of France or President Silvio Berlusconi of Italy? Who will stand when Christ appears? When the Kingdom comes, all these leaders will be set down and a new kind of leadership will rise.

You should not worry about Democracy but start looking for Theocracy instead. You should look for God to set up His Kingdom, for the scripture says, "For unto us, a child is born and unto us a son is given and a government shall be on his shoulders. And he shall be called Wonderful Counselor, Mighty God, Prince of Peace, the Everlasting Father. And of the increase of His government of peace there shall be no end."

You have a major role to play in the setting up of that government and the establishment of His Kingdom, for Jesus said, "The Kingdom is within you." If the Kingdom of God is within you, why is there so much hell coming out of you?

Your nature is the birth of the Kingdom, the nature in which you are created. The Holy Qur'an says, "Set your face for religion, being upright, the nature made by God in which He has created man." Your nature is to live upright. Once that nature is quickened in you, you begin to cast off the Satanic mind and spirit that now inhabits you. That is why Jesus had to cast devils out from among the people.

The first Adam was made from the "dust of the earth," but the second Adam was made of a "quickening spirit." "Quickening" means that life had to be given to the essence of the human being. Once the nature of righteousness in that person is quickened to life, then out of him will come the Kingdom of God.

In the Masonic tradition, Hiram was a master architect. He had plans in his head for the building of the temple, but 15 ruffians conspired on Hiram. Twelve recanted, leaving Jubila, Jubilo and Jubilum, and they hit Hiram in his head and carried him on a westerly course. They buried him in the northern country in a shallow grave, and a man came to raise him, but he did not have the right grip. Then along came One with the Master Grip, which was a lion's paw and He raised him from the dead.

The Bible says, "There's a lion asleep in Judah, but who will wake him?" You are a lion, but you are acting like a pussycat, because you are asleep in the real power of who you are. You are the righteous, the people of God, but you are covered over with the filth of this world's life.

The Book says we were born in sin and shaped in iniquity. Paul said that sin is transgression of the law. We were born in a house that, whatever God says, "Thou shall not do," our rulers and masters say, "It's OK." We have done it all opposite of God.

So, the spirit in us needs to be quickened to life. If Jesus was raised from the dead, the death that he was under was the same death that we are under. He needed his spirit quickened to life, but once the spirit and nature of him was touched by the Word from God, he arose.

***

The Bible says, "A virgin shall conceive." Every virgin that conceives was, after conception, no longer a virgin. But it is wonderful to be a virgin before you conceive. This is not only referring to a female who is a virgin, but it is also talking about a people who had never known a man. The people are like a female virgin, because once you know a man and that man comes to you with truth, then out of a virgin, you will conceive and leadership that is Divine will come forward.

That is why the slave-master wanted to keep you a virgin people—like virgin territory is uncultivated, undeveloped, and raw. Whenever you would give birth to a leader, they found an excuse to kill him, to get rid of him, especially if he was impactful. But when God decides to make a virgin conceive, it is done in an immaculate manner.

You are the virgin that will conceive and—as Moses was brought up out of water and Jesus was raised out of a dead people—so will you be raised from your condition. Once these demons are cast out of you and the real you manifests, then out of your heart, mind and soul will come the Kingdom of God.

The enemy watches all of us, because he understands that it is only through careful watching that he could prevent our destiny. After the crucifixion of Jesus, they laid him in a tomb. Every city where you live is a graveyard. You call it a ghetto, but the scripture calls it a tomb, and you are dead in the tomb.

You may be the majority in your city, but you are like dust, without any social, economic, or political weight. They move you about like dust. If they do not want you in this community, they simply make laws and push you right out. You are in a grave, Black man and woman, and you must be raised from that grave.

The Bible says a stone was placed in front of the tomb and a centurion or a guard was placed outside the stone. But when somebody is in a tomb, why would you need to put a stone in front of the entry and then a guard in front of the stone?

What are you expecting to happen? In the Bible, the guard fell asleep. When he woke up, the stone had been rolled away and the one they thought was dead was gone. In the church, we sing, "The devil is mad and I'm so glad that he missed the soul that he thought he had." How did you escape what he had you in? You cannot do it on your own. The angel of the Lord has to come and roll the stone away, so that you will come forward a new people.

You cannot become new in yourself or in your pastor or in your so-called leader; you can only become new in God. Paul said, "Be ye not conformed to this world, be ye transformed by the renewing of your mind." During slavery, White people made the mind that we have today. We were educated in his mind, so that we keep on doing the slave-master's bidding, knowingly and unknowingly.

A drive-by shooter functions from the mind made by the slave-master. A pimp functions from the mind made by the slave-master. A whore functions from the mind made by the slave-master. A gang-banger who kills his brother who is not wearing the "right" color or using the "right" sign, functions from the mind made by the slave-master.

But you cannot have your mind renewed by somebody who is in the image and likeness of the master. You can only have your mind renewed by one whose spirit has been quickened and whose spirit is demonstrative that he has a new mind that is of God.

***

How did our people get made so that we cannot seem to unite? We know we need to unite in order to get out of the condition that we are in, but we cannot seem to unite. We have had many great leaders, and like the bones in the valley pictured in Ezekiel, we heard the leader, and the bones shook. But they never stood up because the spirit was not in them. That was the grip that was insufficient to raise the bones up.

When they brought our fathers into slavery, they had to first break us from our natural self and make us into a people that would always be their slaves. A slave-trader, a slave-maker, and then a slave-master that will continue to master the slave ad infinitum—until someone comes to interfere with the process that made us negroes, and what we presently are—which is a caricature of who we really are.

Each one of you will lay down in your bed at night and dream about your own greatness and then wake up to the reality that you cannot, or have not been able to, manifest what you know is within yourself. So, all of us are in pain, pain. Our women are hurting because there is no real man in their lives. And we, men, are in pain trying to be a man in a world with a slave-master that denies us manhood. How did this happen?

A man named Willie Lynch, who was a plantation owner in the Caribbean, came to Virginia in 1712. As a result of slave revolts, slave-masters were hanging slaves, but that was bad for business. On his way to deliver his speech, Willie Lynch could smell the rotting carcass of a slave that was hanging from a tree nearby and he said, "You all are doing this thing wrong. You are killing your profit. But I have a foolproof plan that, if you use it, you will produce a perpetual slave."

Like an axis that will turn them continually through the generations, if the slave-masters used his plan, Willie Lynch assured them that the slaves would continue to be under their control for at least 300 years and possibly for 1,000. We are in year 2005. Willie Lynch gave the slave-masters his protocol in 1712, almost 300 years ago—and we are not the product of Jesus Christ, we are the product of Willie Lynch. Although we may be in church, mosque, lodge, we are the product of Willie Lynch.

Willie Lynch outlined a number of differences among the slaves that he manipulated to make his slaves bicker. He also used three things to control his slaves: fear, distrust, and envy. With these three controlling factors, he said the slaves will always be controlled. He started with age, to divide the old from the young. Is there a generational gap today? Yes. Willie Lynch is still in power.

He used color to divide his slaves. When we came from Africa, we were very Black in the color of our skin. Willie Lynch said to take a White sperm to the Blackest women among the slaves, who will then produce sperm that is brown. When more white sperm is introduced to the brown sperm, he would make children a little lighter in color.

He would continue this process until he would produce children with complexions close enough to white, where they could pass for White people. Then, he would put the slaves against each other, making them believe that the lightest ones are the best of them, because they are closest to his color. Is Willie Lynch still in power? Are we still divided by color? Yes.

Then Willie Lynch used intelligence to divide his slaves. Those of us who graduate from college believe we are much better than those of us in the ghetto who did not even graduate from high school. Then, he used size to divide his slaves, so the little nigger will always look to the big nigger and wish he could be big. He also divided male against female and used the size of plantations to divide the slaves, who would boast of their superiority based on the size of their master's plantation. He divided us by hair, coarse from fine. So, we have even given hair a moral quality. If straight hair is good hair, nappy hair is bad hair.

Then Willie Lynch said, "We divide the slave by the status of the slave on the plantation." Today, some of us boast of having dinner with the governor. Willie Lynch is still working in 2005. Then, he used "the attitude of the owner toward the slave" to divide us, and today some of us wish to emulate those Black people who are near to our enemies. Then, he divided those who lived in the valley and those who lived on the hill, then the East, West, North and South.

Today, we have East Coast rappers divided against West Coast rappers, and rappers in the South against those in the Midwest. Willie Lynch is still working. You are the same people, bit by the same snake and suffering from the same condition, but you hate one another because somebody comes from the West, the East, the South, the North, the Caribbean, or Africa. They have divided us in every way possible and it is still working today. The worst element of Willie Lynch's plan is his protocol: "We must take their minds but keep their bodies."

I am making an appeal to all those who want to be a part of the Millions More Movement, to develop the kind of attitude we must have in order to be in the room with people with whom we have disagreement.

Everybody that is on this rostrum here with me does not mean they agree with everything that I say, but there is a cause bigger than our disagreements — and that is the suffering of our people. All of us are in our camps, but Noah had more animals in the ark than he had humans. He was instructed to bring two of every kind and put them in the ark, then get in with his children. So, I said to myself that I need to build a tent big enough for all of the animals to get in.

None of us are really human yet. We are less than human because we have not mastered the humus—the flesh, the blood, the bone that comes from the earth. We are dictated by our bodies rather than letting our minds dictate to our bodies. We are possessed with a carnal mind. The word "carnal" comes from the Latin root, *carnus*, which means "meat."

We are carnal in that the flesh dictates to the mind. So, we have to build a tent big enough that the animals can come in and we set up a system that begins to organize and raise them to humanity, so that when we land on dry land and the ark opens, animals won't come out, but a new creature in God will come forth.

There is no future for us unless this process is reversed. Anybody who would reverse this process is dangerous to the slave-master. So our enemies watch for leadership coming up among us, and anyone who would reverse this process they consider an enemy.

Frederick Douglass was an enemy; David Walker was an enemy; Marcus Garvey, Noble Drew Ali were all enemies. Huey Newton and the Black Panther Party tried to reverse Willie Lynch's madness, and that's why the enemy came against the Panthers. The enemy would strip the Panthers naked and walk them out of their offices among their community naked to teach the women you cannot depend on Black men.

Those of us who are practicing manhood are endangering their process, so they have to speak evil of those of us who are trying to be men and they do not want the Black woman falling in love with the Black man. So, Black women were made to love, trust, and fear the White man for what he could do.

Black women were like putty in his hands, and he could use you, although you did not know, to break your man. When Black women marry Black men, they fall in love because they think we are what we are not. But when they become disappointed for choosing their husbands, they are angry and use their tongues to cut us down.

That is the new bullwhip. Black women are beating Black men down because he was made like that by our enemy, but Black women do not know how to unmake what the enemy has done, so they seek to destroy it with their mouth.

We have become each other's enemy. We could get up out of hell and make a better woman, a better man, a better people, and reverse Willie Lynch. Let us build God's Kingdom on earth.

7

The Least of These My Brethren

We are here in Richmond to promote the 10th anniversary of the Million Man March and to inform the community of why we feel there is a need for a Millions More Movement. Ten years ago, we called for one million Black men to come to Washington.

Nearly two million came, not to demand something from the government, but to ask God's forgiveness for our failure to be the men, husbands, fathers, providers, protectors of our women and children, and builders of communities as we believe we should and could be. It was for us, a time of atonement, reconciliation, and the acceptance of responsibility to change the realities of Black family relations and life.

We were blessed on that day. As a result of that day, 25,000 orphans found homes, prisoners were adopted, the crime and murder rates went down throughout the communities of Black people. Many Black men paid child support for their families that they had forsaken, mentoring programs were started, entrepreneurs came out of the March to build businesses.

Some of the Local Organizing Committees remained faithful to the ideas promoted, and many in that audience joined churches, mosques, synagogues, and organizations that we asked them to join.

Many people asked, "Where did the money go?" I promised on the Mall that I would give an audit, and within three months, three CPA firms gave an audit of every nickel and dime. We went back to Washington and held a press conference, but the country did not get that message. That audit is on our website at www.millionsmoremovement.com and you can download it and see where every nickel, dime and dollar went.

Ten years later, although we have many more Black people with BA, MA, and doctorate degrees, many more Black entrepreneurs, Black men and women in public service and politics, many more millionaires and a few billionaires, but the masses of our people are slipping further and further behind.

So, for the first time in our history, all Black leaders and organizations across the whole spectrum of Black thought met in Washington, D.C. at a press conference held at the National Press Club (on May 2, 2005), and agreed to work together. The horrific condition of the masses of our people demanded that we come together and work out a programmatic thrust that the learned of our people can connect their skills to the problems of our people.

Then, by pooling our resources intellectually and financially, we might be able to build our people up from where we are. We believe that we can no longer depend on a compassionate, benevolent president to solve our problems, for at best, we have always been voting for the lesser of two evils. So, we have decided that we want to be good for ourselves and so we are accepting that responsibility.

October 14 will be a Day of Absence, October 15 will be the mass gathering, and October 16 will be a commemoration of the Day of Atonement, where all of us will fill the religious institutions in our cities to make that covenant with God that we talked about 10 years ago, which reads: *"If my people which are called by My Name shall humble themselves and pray, and seek my face and turn from their wicked ways, then will I hear from heaven, forgive their sins and heal their land."* (I Corinthians 7:14)

This land is sick. Our world is sick. Our people are sick. We need a healing that none of our scholars are able to produce. God's Promise is real, but there is something that we must do in order for God to fulfill His Word. We have had many, many broken promises from our government and leaders, but God never fails in fulfilling His Promise. He has said that, before one jot or tittle of His Word would fail, the heavens and the earth would pass away.

So, the covenant that we want is a covenant with God, a covenant with each other, and a covenant with our people that we will work as never before in a unified way to solve the many problems of our people.

We are inviting our Brothers and Sisters in the Latino community, because they are our family and we have similar issues. Where there are similar issues, we need to form strategic alliances for economic and political power. We are inviting our Native American family and the poor of our people, for when all of us unite, organize, mobilize, and strategize, then we can make America a country of the people, by the people and truly for the people.

Thank you and, at this time, I will accept your questions.

Is the Nation of Islam going to do anything to help the people who were hit hard by Hurricane Katrina?

Minister Farrakhan: Yes, sir. The Millions More Movement, which is a united front of all of our organizations, we are calling all of us together to pool our resources to address the specific concerns of those who FEMA and the Red Cross are not servicing. There are many mayors who have contacted me from little cities and towns of Mississippi that no representative of the Red Cross or FEMA has touched. So, we are going to do our best to service those communities.

We are getting the preachers and leaders of organizations together because we feel that the time is now to really act on the principles that Jesus Christ and Muhammad taught. Muhammad taught that, if you have a bowl of soup and your Brother had none, half of your bowl belongs to your Brother. Jesus the Christ said, when the disciples asked him, "Master when were you hungry and we fed you not, when were you naked and we clothed you not, when were you out of doors and we gave you not shelter and when were you imprisoned and we ministered not unto you?" he said, "Inasmuch as you have not done these things to the least of these my brethren, you have not done it also unto me."

New Orleans, Mississippi and Alabama are a disaster, where the least of these are homeless, hungry, and without clothes and shelter, sick and need to be ministered unto. So, we are calling on all the churches and mosques to open their doors. If you have to put cots in the basements of your churches, go and get the people that Jesus and Muhammad talked about, and put them in your churches. Feed, clothe, shelter, and educate them, and give them a new start.

We are asking all of us, Muslims and Christians, to go to the relief centers and adopt a family and take that family to your home and minister unto them as Jesus would have us to do and share that bowl of soup with them as Muhammad would have us to do.

Then, out of the darkness of this tragedy will come the light of love and brotherhood, and a new people will emerge with trust, love, and confidence because we did not talk about what Jesus and Muhammad said, we acted on it. In acting on those principles, the tragedy will turn into triumph.

In your address (to Richmond on Sept. 4), will you talk about the government's response or lack of response to the crisis in the Gulf Coast region?

Minister Farrakhan: My sadness is that we all watched the *Weather Channel*, *MSNBC*, *FOX*, and *CNN*. We watched Katrina grow from a Category 1 storm and come into the Gulf and build from a 1 to a 3, and paused. It was moving quite slowly. When it was understood that it was going to be a category 4 and then a 5, that was the time that FEMA should have been activated and trucks should

A REASON TO UNITE

have been sent to the area. Most of the people who could not get out was not because they did not want to, but because they did not have the means to get out. But if those trucks had been there in a timely fashion, we might have been able to save many, many, many more lives.

In the horror of that tragedy, you cannot bring the Ten Commandments to bear when self-preservation is the first law of nature. We are animals until we are made into human beings. When human conditions do not prevail, the animal in the human takes over. Naturally, if a person breaks into a place to get food, we can understand that.

We cannot understand taking a television when there is no place to plug it in or no one to sell it to. We cannot countenance the rape of innocent people. This is a horror, but we need to be on the ground to feel what they are feeling, sense what they are sensing and feel the despair and hopelessness that many of them felt. If we had acted better, maybe it would have been better. New Orleans may present the template for how to best prepare for the next city—and there will be more and there will be more.

I have sadness, but I am also glad that President (George) Bush was on the ground to see the horror, devastation, bodies floating in the water, snakes coming out of their hiding places, and alligators and now pestilence is on the horizon. Why do I say that it is good that our president was on the ground? Because Jesus said, "As a man soweth, the same shall he also reap."

Our government is in error. The war in Iraq—supposedly because Saddam Hussein had weapons of mass destruction—was an error. It was an intentional departure from the truth. Policy was already made, and facts were arranged to fit the policy. Nearly 2,000 children of American families are dead, and thousands wounded, and bodies destroyed for the rest of their lives.

I remember Secretary of Defense (Donald) Rumsfeld saying, when the bombs were falling on Iraq, and the newspapers reporting the "shock and awe" from the power of America on a country that could not defend its own air space. Now, we in America could not defend our air space from Katrina. When you look at the devastation, they say it was like a bomb dropped.

For God's sake, see what we are suffering and see the suffering that we have visited on others. Stop it now before the God of Justice brings more natural disasters. You cannot arrest Him as a terrorist, but He is terrorizing America today.

We must change. Our government must give better guidance and better direction, stop lying and deceiving the American people and maybe God will be merciful and hold back the four winds that are now blowing on this great nation.

Do you feel the faith-based money is jeopardizing the concept of church and state?

Minister Farrakhan: It is a use of funds to co-opt church to make the church the vassal of the state. Slowness to adopt the Movement on the Mall in Washington, that can be forgiven. Slowness to involve yourself in that which will save our people cannot be forgiven.

We are not going anywhere without the church. It is a valuable instrument in the salvation of our people, but it must not be the playground of the Bush administration or any administration. In order for the church to be free to do its job, it must be free to say to the kings and rulers of the world, "Thus sayeth the Lord." If the church is taking money from the government, then the church finds it difficult to be a critical voice to correct the government.

God sends prophets. We respect kings and bow to the kings, but we do not obey the kings when they give an instruction that is against what "Thus sayeth the Lord." So, prophets, apostles, and ministers must never be prostitutes.

We are the servants of God and, therefore, we serve the best interests of government, not by yielding to the misdirection of government, but by correcting the direction of government so that the government can never do to the American people what this government unfortunately has done in the war in Iraq. The war has caused the rape of the treasuries of nearly $340 billion, some of which could have been used, but was denied, in New Orleans to build the levees. A Category 5 hurricane would never have destroyed that city if the government had invested in that infrastructure.

Our priorities are disturbed. Our priority is warfare. The budget for war is criminal and the budget to cultivate the American people educationally is going down. With all the beautiful buildings that we build, if we do not spend money to build human beings, then the savagery of humans will tear down and destroy the beauty of your material buildings.

The greatest resource of this country is its people, but they are being purposely dumbed down so they can be easily led like sheep, while a small group ruling, deceiving, and taking the wealth of the many in the name of globalization. America has to rethink where this country is going.

I am one Brother that will always be found saying, "Thus sayeth the Lord." If you let me out of prison, I will be able to help, but I am locked in a prison of public opinion that has been created by the media; I am called anti- everything. From my prison, I wrote a letter to Pres. Bush, which you can download on www.finalcall.com, I warned him in 2001 that I knew what was in his mind and I warned him that if he (goes to war in Iraq) that you are going to run into something that you and those with you have not considered and it will be your undoing.

Now, his ratings are going down. I wrote him a second letter and told him that every body of an American serviceperson that dies will be laid at his door. Cindy Sheehan is just the tip of the iceberg. There are many wounded families that are in deep pain because they do not mind sacrificing their lives if the country is really threatened.

But to use these young men and women's lives on the basis of what is false with manipulated evidence that those at the top knew was a lie—that is a high crime and a misdemeanor for which the government should be set down, and something new and better put in its place, lest a government like this lead the American people fully into the Chastisement of God.

I said, three months ago, that God was going to take one American city and take it all the way down to show America that what you do to others, it will come back to you. This arrogant leadership must be made humble. When you fly Air Force One over the devastated area, if God's Wrath does not humble you enough to see that there is more where that came from, then you do not deserve to be the leader of the greatest nation on earth.

Are you saying that this nation's engagement in the war in Iraq led to the hurricane hitting New Orleans and the Gulf Coast and taking lives?

Minister Farrakhan: No, I am speaking of America's evil. Most of you are very unaware of what your government does in the name of the American people to make nations fall. I am talking about killing millions of people. The American people know nothing about America's foreign policy.

If you travel the earth and see the suffering in the world due to America's policies; these people do not hate America because we are free; they hate America for the policies that have sucked and siphoned the wealth of nations so that we could be a wealthy people, while in Africa they are living on less than a dollar a day. We must pay for these things. That is why Jesus said, "As a man soweth, the same shall he also reap." So, our government must be careful of what seeds it sows.

I am suggesting that the hurricane and the disaster it brought to (the Gulf Coast region) is only the beginning of sorrows. What about pestilence, famine, and earthquakes? This is what Jesus foretold.

You can run all over the world and find terrorists; go find the God Who is terrorizing this land and arrest Him. That you cannot do, so the best thing for us to do is recognize the power of God has entered this house. You will find unusual rain, snow, wind, and earthquakes. Everything you depend on for your sustenance is going to be turned against you. You must pay for what you have done; we all must pay for what we have done, and it seems like its pay day.

Would you, on a personal level, like to send a personal message (to the victims of Hurricane Katrina)?

    Minister Farrakhan: It is bigger than a person or a personal message. The people do not need messages, they need help. All of us who have not suffered what New Orleans suffered, we can reach for those evacuees. This would turn a tragedy into a triumph: a triumph of the will, a triumph of the spirit of the human and it would cause all of us to rise above our selfishness and materialist nature to become human.

    Then, God can look at us and remove some of His Wrath. This is the standard that God uses to measure nations. America has a beautiful heart; it is just misguided.

8

As A Man Soweth,
So Shall He Also Reap

I am honored by God to have the privilege of serving in an hour like this. The scripture says that we would enter a time of trouble like there never was since there was a time and a nation. In that hour, Michael, the Archangel, would stand for his people. I do not know who that is, but I do know that we have to stand for our people in this hour.

The tragedy of Hurricane Katrina affecting our Brothers and Sisters in Louisiana, Alabama and Mississippi is a great trial for them, but it is also a trial for us. Allah (God) says in the Holy Qur'an that when you are a believer in God and a misfortune befalls the believer, he or she says, "Allah (God) is my patron and to Him is my eventual return."

No one comes to this world and escapes misfortune. It is by the means of misfortune that the hearts of the righteous are tried. The Bible says, "The Lord giveth and the Lord taketh away, but blessed is the name of the Lord."

In the Holy Qur'an, Allah (God) says to His servant, Muhammad, "Surely I am going to try you with something of fear, hunger, loss of property, loss of life and diminution of fruits, but give good news to those who are patient and steadfast under trial." In another verse, it reads: "Allah loves those who are patient and steadfast under trial."

Our Brothers and Sisters and the people in the Gulf Coast were tried with fear; when they knew that a Category 5 hurricane was going to strike where they lived. Certainly, many of the evacuees were hungry. They were breaking into stores to find food and nourishment. "Thou shalt not steal" is on hold when the first law of nature is self-preservation.

So, one can understand breaking into a place that has food and you have none for you and your children. Self-preservation says the food in that store belongs to you if you can get to it. Human beings start as animals and then we rise to humans. The highest level of human development is the reflection of Divine. When everything is lost, the degenerative process begins. Once you are deprived of what it takes to be human to reflect the Divine, then the animal in the human manifests itself.

Our trial is comfort: We will go home and, God willing, we will have a meal on our tables, a roof over our heads, and food in our refrigerators and a place to sleep, while our Brothers and Sisters have none. The question is, "What are we going to do about it?" Muslims, Christians, and Jews say, "God is Love," but we cannot talk today. It is not "Well-said thy good and faithful servant, enter into thy joy"—it is "well done." So, the test now is what are we going to do?

Prophet Muhammad (Peace be upon him) said, "If you have a bowl of soup and your Brother has none, then half of your bowl belongs to your Brother." That means your Brother has a right to half your bowl. He expects it from you, if you say you are truly his Brother.

If I do not belong to the same "sect" of religion as you, then maybe I cannot claim half of your bowl of soup, so then you will have a way of holding on to your bowl. That is why some members of our Christian family do not answer calls to join us. Some may say, "I am a Christian and he is a Muslim, and I am not going to waste my time going to something called by a Muslim."

But God used me ... but let us say that you do not know that God used me. Let us say that I am a vain Negro and I called for a million men to come to Washington, D.C. 10 years ago for the Million Man March. The call was different.

We have been here for over 450 years and have never heard of a White man, much less a Black man, call the children of slaves off the plantation. It has never been done since we have been here. The call was unique.

On October 16, 1995, we saw Black men wall to wall, front to back, standing for 14 hours, in a measure of peace that had never been seen before in America or anywhere else in the world. How can you say that the call was not of God. I do not have the power to make those men respond to my call, but a God could touch their hearts and make them respond.

Christians, how are you going to explain their response, since you believe that you are the close ones to God, because I have a different label than you? I did something that none of you could do, yet you believe that God is closer to you than He is to me. The logic is not right.

You have been listening to vain people all of your life—vain people, with vainglorious imaginations to exalt themselves, instead of exalting God, truth, or the masses of our suffering people. That is not Farrakhan.

Most Christian pastors know that I preach Jesus. Why can't you walk with me? I am not asking you to lift me. I am asking you to unite so that we can lift a people who are dying in our face. The enemy has always controlled us through fear, distrust, and envy.

When I made the call for the Million Man March, some asked, "Why him, why not me?" The Holy Qur'an says that Allah (God) knows best where to place His message. If He did not place it on you and placed it on me, then you should respect God's choice.

You are a difficult people, but you are headed for the worst whipping that any people ever received since God sent prophets into the world. I cannot keep you from your whipping. I love you and I will give my life for you, but I cannot keep you from the whipping that you are about to receive. You have played with God, Allah, Jehovah, Yahweh, or whatever name you call Him. You have played with Jesus and used his name as a marketing tool to feather nests and fatten pocketbooks, but you are not saving people.

Jesus never built one church or synagogue; that is our vanity, so that preachers can boast of their greatness. Jesus was in the highways and byways where the people were. The words of Jesus can be translated to apply to, not only the church, but also the mosque and synagogue, when he described the church as "whited sepulchers, in them are bones of dead men." Do you think that we do not have to pay a price for our hypocrisy?

Jesus also said, "As a man soweth, the same shall he also reap." America has sown a lot of bad seeds. The presidents of the United States have been the stewards of wicked policies that have hurt the weak and the poor in the house and slaughtered the weak and the poor outside of the house. This is real. Open your eyes. This is a wicked nation.

John the Revelator said Babylon is fallen because it has become the habitation of devils, a hole for every foul spirit and a cage for every unclean and hateful bird. The prophets were not talking about ancient Babylon, but a mystery Babylon. It was a golden chalice on the outside, but filth and abomination were on the inside. The gold on the outside is so attractive, but inside is filth and abomination. That is the same way that the human being is today.

You spend time washing the outside but have no time cleaning up the inside. We spend time dressing up the outside, but we do not spend time dressing up the inside. We look good on the outside, but on the inside, like Babylon, is filth and abomination of every kind. So, we have earned the chastisement of God.

As it is in ancient time, God sends a messenger to stand between His Wrath and the people. When I think about my Brother Pastors, whom I love, and think about what they think about me—not because they think that I am a bad person, they know better—I know that they are afraid because they think they will lose some benefit from the enemy.

But how can you be a man of God and be afraid of the modern Caesar or modern Pharoah? When you are afraid, then you do the will of what you are afraid of. The Bible says that the beginning of wisdom is the fear of God. If it is God that you fear, then you bow down to His Will. If it is Pharoah or Caesar that you fear, then you bow down to their will because you are afraid of losing some advantage.

You are afraid of standing with me because you fear that the government will watch you like they watch me. Why is the United States government watching me? I do not lie, steal, rob or rape, so why are they watching me? They watched Noah, Lot, Abraham, Moses, Daniel, and everybody that threatens wicked rule. They watched Jesus; so, if you are a true disciple of Jesus and they are not watching you, then you need to examine whether you are a true disciple of Jesus.

President George Bush made a terrible blunder, and his administration made a terrible blunder. Allah (God) was merciful with Hurricane Katrina. When she came to the southern coast of Florida as a category 1 hurricane, as a tropical storm, she did some damage. She then moved to the Gulf, slowly traveled north, and began building up to a Category 3 hurricane and stayed in the Gulf for a while.

The government had time to do something, even if they could not move trucks all the way into the area. They knew the hurricane was on a course to hit New Orleans. When she became a Category 4 hurricane and the winds hit 150 mph, they said it was headed for New Orleans, but not a truck moved.

Nobody moved. I assumed that Pres. Bush has a television. I assumed that the president of FEMA has a television. When Hurricane Katrina struck, some said that they busted the levees. I do not know how true that is, but I know that White people have done worse than that. The youth today do not know anything about this enemy, because grandparents did not tell their children about the evil of the people that we have been living among in this country. So the youth think it is a party going on and you think they have changed.

However, we know the reality, as elders, but have we told our children or have we gone to sleep on a pacifier, because we can now eat in a White man's restaurant or sleep in a White man's hotel, yet put our hotels and restaurants out of business? You are nothing more in America than a commodity, and a useless commodity at that.

Brothers and Sisters, you are useless to the White man, and he does not have any jobs for you. In slavery, there was full employment; everybody had a job. Everyone had something to eat, even though we ate low off the hog, and we wore cheap clothes. Now we wear the best clothes yet are the worst people in our self-hatred and the destruction of our people. We never did anything like this in the darkest days of slavery.

Women are looking like prostitutes, because the stylists are taking our women's clothes off them. Every time you take a woman down, you take the nation down. If you want the nation to go up, you lift the woman. We have become a nation of dogs and our language reflects what we have become.

I am hurting because we have come to a very dark time in America's history, our history and world history. As a man soweth, the same shall he also reap. You love White people, but they have given you nothing but hell. The government is wicked.

When they wanted to take the possessions of the Spanish in the western hemisphere—Cuba, Puerto Rico and the Hawaiian islands—they manufactured a rationale to go to war. Americans blew up a ship, the US Maine, in Cuban waters, killing Americans to justify the Spanish-American War. At the end of that war, Cuba, Puerto Rico, and Hawaii were in the hands of America. These are the people who plan death and destruction to further their political and economic ends— don't you know that yet?

When President John Kennedy was in office, Cuban President Fidel Castro overthrew the Batiste regime, which was the pawn of the U.S. government. Pres. Castro then shared the wealth of Cuba with its peasantry, and America has feared Cuba ever since. Members of the Joint Chiefs-of-Staff met with Pres. Kennedy to propose blowing up a ship, killing Americans, blaming it on Cuba, in order to send U.S. troops into Cuba.

He rejected it, but the thought of warmongering rules the government. The minute a poor man, Hugo Chavez, rose to power in Venezuela and took control of the oil, the Bush administration planned a coup and took him from power—but several days later, the poor put Pres. Chavez back into office.

Why do you think Jesus said it is easier for a camel to go through the eye of a needle than it is for a rich man to enter the kingdom of heaven? It is because rich people are rich because they suck the blood of the poor, and any man who would awaken the poor becomes the enemy of the rich who control political and economic power. That is why Jesus had to be crucified—because the poor listened to him gladly.

God is angry with America, but He is also displeased with you, because you have been playing with God. Do you think that the money that you throw in the collection plate as charity can save you when God starts judging? What God promised, He is now bringing on America and Pres. Bush's policies have brought it to America's doors.

9

We Must Reflect
Jesus The Revolutionary

It is wonderful to be a servant of God and a servant of the people. In the Bible, Jesus said it beautifully: "He who would be chief among you let him be your servant." Black people have been trained on how to serve the White man, but it takes God to touch our hearts to make us servants of one another.

Our people need service. They do not need masters, they need servers, and I am honored that in my lifetime I am being blessed to see what I have longed to see since I was a little boy: the unity of us, as a people. How joyous my heart is to be with my Christian family. I told White Arabs that I would not jump over one Black Christian to find unity with a White Arab, even though they are Muslims and I am a Muslim.

The church is my family. I had a Christian upbringing; I sang in the choir; I carried the cross; I know all the hymns of my church. Sometimes, on Sunday morning while I am changing channels on my television, I hear some of those hymns that I used to sing and I sing quietly to myself and tears fall from my eyes, because I remember my church. There is no power that will separate me from the church, even though I say that I am a Muslim.

Without the church, our people are lost. The church has been our comfort when we had nothing to hold on to. The corruptors are always busy corrupting the church, mosque, and synagogue, so that the house of God is a divided house. Satan is really the master today of Islam, Christianity, and Judaism.

We hold up the names of Christ, Muhammad, and Moses as a shield for the way we live, which is totally opposite of what these men lived and the life that they taught us to live—which says that Satan caused us to deviate even though we claim the great names of our prophets. So, religion, as Karl Marx said, did become the opiate of the people.

The Honorable Elijah Muhammad was the son and grandson of Baptist preachers. When he would sit in the church in Sandersville, Georgia, listening to his father, he knew that one day he would preach something different, but he did not know what it was.

When he met Master Fard Muhammad and heard what Master Fard Muhammad taught, he began preaching what is called "Islam." His work in setting up mosques was a protest against the church. It was not that Jesus was off the mark; it was that we were off the mark in the name of Jesus. He taught us wisdom and never allowed music in the temple; the music was to be the Word of God.

He cleaned us up by teaching the Bible, not the Holy Qur'an. When we came to him, we were like everybody else—liars, thieves, adulterers, murderers and then some—but he used the Bible to call us to live a righteous life. He called us to live the lives of the prophets, whose names we honored with our tongues, but our lives were far removed from them.

When I saw his temple and met Brother Minister Malcolm X, he became my mentor. He was one of the finest examples that I could have ever had in my beginning days in Islam. I never heard him curse. He was never late for an appointment. When I would sleep in his house, he would wake me up at 5 a.m. for Fajr prayer.

He was an exceedingly disciplined man under the Teachings of the Honorable Elijah Muhammad. The Honorable Elijah Muhammad never liked whooping in the church, so he made all of his ministers like professors; we had to teach and become lovers of knowledge, because our people are in their condition because of a lack of knowledge. Even though Malcolm X did not go beyond the 8th grade, he had genius sitting in his breast—as genius is in the breast of our people. They just need to be quickened to life.

When Malcolm awakened, he began reading everything in the library worth reading, starting with the dictionary, from cover to cover. Whenever I would sit to be taught by Brother Malcolm, he always broke words down into their meanings; he understood the root of words. He knew that, through words, you can either get tricked or you can be free.

The first book he put in my hands was "100 Amazing Facts about the Negro" by J.A. Rogers; then "100 Years of Lynching," then "17 Million Negroes, 17 Million Dollars." I had to read all of those books, study my Lessons. Then, I had to read another book by J.A. Rogers, "From Superman to man." Then, I had to study world history, under his direction. Then, he gave me the Holy Qur'an, the first one that I had ever owned.

The Honorable Elijah Muhammad started a revolution in the church from his own rebellion against the way of the church. Because of him, a Black Theology emerged in the Christian house. Before the Honorable Elijah Muhammad, the African Methodist Episcopal Church was Black conscious. It was the church of Marcus Garvey and many of the revolutionaries. But when the Honorable Elijah Muhammad started teaching us that Jesus was our Brother because he was a Black man, then all of the White images of him came down and we began taking pride in ourselves.

I am so happy to be on the rostrum of this house of God with the head of the Interdenominational Theological Center, because for years we have been at odds, not because we have really been at odds, but because an enemy wants to keep us at odds. If we ever united, we know that the real revolution will take place.

Jesus was a revolutionary. He laid down the path of revolution if you really understand him. He was not a milquetoast man who was sweet and nice. How can we represent that great man in a punkish manner? Jesus is the key to the freedom of every human being who lives on this earth.

Mary, the mother of Jesus, is honored in Islam above all women and above the mothers of all other prophets. Why Mary? Her womb was blessed with a world saviour, a child whose destiny was to perfectly reflect the wisdom, mind, spirit, and power of the Creator of the heavens and the earth. Jesus was the man who would once again lift the human from his degraded state to the exalted state that God created human beings to be.

We must understand Jesus the revolutionary because, if the Millions More Movement does not reflect Jesus the revolutionary, it will never be the effective tool for the redemption, reconciliation—of not only Black people, but all humanity—back to God. From the time of the fall of Adam, the world has needed a human being who could connect mankind, or man, again with God.

Adam's death was not physical; it was spiritual. His fall represented the fall of all humanity. When the human falls, that human (male or female) begins to live in the underworld of his desires. When Adam's eyes came open after his rebellion against God, his eyes became open to the world of passion and appetite from the navel down. Once he fell down to live by his appetite, then greed, lust and covetousness began to take hold of the human mind to degrade the human into a being far less than what God created us to be. He created us in His image and after His likeness.

The Holy Qur'an says that Allah (God) created us to be khalifah, to stand in His place as His successor. You cannot succeed God if you are not god. David the Psalmist said, "Ye are all gods, children of the Most High God." But you first have to be His child. It is an error for preachers to say that we are all the children of God. We all have the capacity to be the child of God, but that is a decision that we have to make as to whose child we are going to be.

The Bible says, "As by one man sin entered into the world and death came by sin." All men have sinned, so all are under death. The Bible also says, "There is a way that seemeth right unto a man, but the ends thereof are the ways of death." What kind of death?

Once human beings live in the flesh rather than in the spirit, they become dead to the real power of self. You do not need a television to see or a telephone to hear, when you are alive in the spirit of God as Jesus was, and is. The Bible says, "Jesus, knowing their thoughts, did..." He did not have to have a telephone to listen—like the government uses to listen; they are trying to imitate the natural powers of human beings who live in the spirit of God, but they cannot do it from their minds, because they are too wicked.

God allows you to get hints of your powers; sometimes you can see an occurrence before it happens or hear something that you know you were not present to hear. The real ear and eyes are not physical. When your mind is lit with the Light of God, you see beyond the eyes and hear beyond the ears. You are naturally endowed with those powers, but those powers have been put to sleep because we are following a people who live diametrically opposed to the way of the Creator.

In the scripture, Jesus says, "As by one man sin entered into the world, and death came by sin." So, by one man should all be made alive.

If and you were the devil, the archdeceiver, and knew that Jesus was coming to defeat you and your underworld of transgression, who would you have to deceive the world about? Satan knows that Jesus is the end of his world the beginning of a new world. Jesus is a door. He said, "If you enter into me, you will be saved."

Jesus described himself in many ways:

"I am the true vine and my Father is the husbandman."

"I am the bread of life."

"I am the light of the world."

"I am the way, the truth and the life."

"I am the good shepherd."

The good shepherd lays down his life for his sheep. A man like that is a man who the whole world needs. A man like that can raise us up out of the condition that we are in and raise us up again to become beings that reflect God. The human being is only a stage of development; you have to grow from the level of an animal to be a human, which means that you have mentally evolved to be able to put the humus (the earth) under the power of a resurrected mind. But that process of evolution and development does not stop with a human being; it continues until you become a divine being reflecting the perfection of the Creator.

That is why Jesus said, "I go to prepare a place for you, that where I am you may be also." The Bible also says that "they will be changed in the twinkling of an eye" and "they will be like him, Jesus." The Bible says that Jesus was exalted to the "right hand of God" and given power over everything except God, Himself.

Jesus serves as an example that a human being, born of a woman, could master the forces of the universe, in order to show us our possibilities, that we should never accept what the world has made us; we must be willing to accept what God wants to make us, through Jesus, a revolutionary.

A real revolution is not with the gun; a real revolution is to overthrow the government in your mind. You must ask yourself, who is the king in your dome? Then, you will know whose children you are. If we are the body of Christ, then our hands do the work of Jesus, our mouths speak the will and the word of Jesus, and our feet walk the path of Jesus. But whose children are we?

Satan has performed a magnificent act of deception. The Bible says he would make himself an angel of light. He knows God because that is the only way that he can deceive us about God. You can be a dumb devil—and most of us are just dumb devils—but Satan is a devil-maker. He is wise because he knows how to manipulate people to make them think that they are on the path of God, while they have actually strayed from the straight way. So, the Bible says, "We war not against flesh and blood but against principalities and powers and the rulers of the darkness of this world and spiritual wickedness in high places."

It would take years to fully teach this subject, because Jesus is so dynamic a human being. I walk in the path of Jesus. There is no other path for a true revolutionary. A true revolutionary rises up not necessarily from the finest of circumstances, for Jesus was born in an ox stall, so he was born among animals. I walk the path of Jesus, which is not an easy path. Who is arrayed against me?

We live in a modern Rome. Ancient Rome, Sodom and Gomorrah, Persia and Babylon are nothing compared to this country. The government of the United States has always been looking like Cain, after he slew his brother Abel. He knew that the blood of Abel was crying out for justice, so he said that, "Every man who sees me will slay me." That is the mind of a guilty person.

America has done so much evil that she sees death coming from everywhere. White people do not believe we have a heart for forgiveness because they know that, if they were in our shoes, they would be plotting to kill them— like this government worked against Dr. Martin Luther King Jr. While they were talking to him in the White House, they were plotting to kill him.

When God gives you revelation, it is your test. If you use the wisdom of God according to the will of God, then you are a child of God. But if you use it to fatten your pockets, then you are the child of Satan, and maybe Satan himself. In the Bible, Revelations 2:9, it reads, "Those who say they are Jews and are not, I will make them of the synagogue of Satan." This is referring to a specific group of people who claim to be Jews, but they are not because they use the wisdom of God for wicked purposes. And there are Christians and Muslims who also use the wisdom of God for wicked purposes.

So, among all of the monotheistic expressions, there is gross hypocrisy. Those who try to do what the prophets say are overshadowed by those who use the names of the prophets to shield unclean practice. In trying to walk this path of Jesus, I have angered that Satanic mind because I am pulling the cover off their deceptive practice.

The scripture says, "Let this mind be in you, the same that was in Christ Jesus." "Let" is a verb of permission, which means we have to accept an invitation. Christ Jesus had the kind of mind that God offered Adam in the Garden of Eden, which he rebelled against—the mind that Jesus offers us is the Mind of God. In order to accept this mind that is offered to us, we have to permit the overthrow of the mind that is in us now. God is calling for a regime change—get rid of the mind of Willie Lynch and accept the Mind of God.

Let the mind of Christ Jesus come into your life. If he knocks, let him in, for if you let him in, He will sup with you. This will make Satan angry, because Jesus came to meddle in the lives of people who thought that they had accepted him but were actually following the mind of Satan. If you let him in, you will be able to say, "Greater is he that is in me than he that is in the world."

Psalms 23 reads, "The Lord is my shepherd"—I have no leader but the Lord; "I shall not want"—for anything that I will not be able to achieve because if He is my shepherd, I can do all things in Christ.

"He leadeth me besides the still waters, he restoreth my soul. He leadeth me in the path of righteousness for his namesake. Yea though I walk in the valley of the shadow of death, I shall fear no evil, for thou art with me. Thy rod and thy staff they comfort me. Thou preparest a table for me in the presence of my enemies. My cup runneth over, surely goodness and mercy shall follow me all the

days of my life and I shall dwell in the house of the Lord forever." This is the Promise of the Lord; this is our inheritance.

Let him in and there is nothing that we will not be able to achieve.

10

On The Road to Discipleship

We have arrived at a time of trouble like there never was since there was a time and a nation. There is no such thing as escaping the Divine Law that governs this creation, the Law of Justice. We may hire a good lawyer, lie our way through a trial, and get away from man in the courts of this world. The enemy may shoot us down and claim that we had a weapon, and his brother judge may rule that it was justifiable, and we leave with grieving hearts. And we, in our ignorance, may shoot one another in foolish fratricidal conflict and go home and live as though nothing has happened.

But for every deed, there is a consequence. No one escapes the Divine Law of Justice. As it is for individuals, so it is for nations. The Holy Qur'an says, "You will see every nation kneeling down before its book and the wicked will say woe is me." The recorder of deeds will not miss anything or anyone.

Every nation writes its record. There are many things that nations do that they hide and seal the records for a set period of time, before it can be revealed to the public. There are many things that individuals hide that we are afraid if such truth comes to light. Many people look good on the surface, but they are wicked on the inside.

America presents itself to the world as a wonderful nation of freedom. The inscription on the Statue of Liberty reads, "Give me your tired, your poor, your huddled masses yearning to breathe free, the wretched refuse of your teeming shores, send these the homeless and tempest tossed to me. I lift my lamp beside the golden door." Jesus could say that, not America.

America is like a golden chalice on the outside, with filth and abomination of every kind on the inside. This is a country that has allowed its citizens to be anything that they wish to be of evil and it is encouraged. It is good that is hated; it is righteousness that is not wanted. When people try to change their life of evil to a life of righteousness, their friends will ask what is wrong with them. Their friends will invite them to return to wrongdoing in order to see if they are strong enough to maintain a righteous posture.

I hope that you will appreciate how difficult it is to tell you the truth and how difficult it is for you to receive the truth because of your fear of your 400-year-old oppressor. It is not him, but your fear of him that keeps you bound to behavioral patterns that make the oppressor happy but make our people unproductive. We suffer from fear to speak truth to power; fear of losing what you do not even have; fear of loss of status of your enemy; fear that maybe the boys downtown will not approve of you for daring to break the chains that bind your minds and hearts.

We will never be free as a people if we continue to fear man as we ought to fear God. When I speak to you, I talk to you as a brother, father, and as one who loves you and is willing to give my life for you to see us free, justified, and equal as a people.

We are on the verge of a great chastisement from God. Although this is a painful truth, we must heed it. We have been playing with God and marketing Jesus like a commodity, but we are unwilling to walk after Jesus. We think that it is sufficient to lift him up in praise. While that is good, the best way to lift Jesus is to follow in his footsteps. He said, "If any man would be my disciple, he must first deny himself."

Denying yourself is denying the things of self that he and the God Who he represents disapproves of. Can you deny yourself the fleshly lusts, the appetites that keep our minds revolving on a low plane, even though you are in church and singing in the choir, or in the mosque preaching the word or bowing down in prayer, or in the synagogue praising Yahweh? When the service is over, we enjoyed the music and word, but they had no power to make us desire to do better with our lives.

"If any man would be my disciple, he must first deny himself." All of the prophets taught fasting. Why does God want you to deny yourself food? If you can step away from food—which is natural—and water—which is life itself—then you can step away from lying, cheating, and discipline your sexual appetites to be a non-fornicator or non-adulterer. So God may ask us to fast in order to build your discipline. What God really wants us to deny is the evil that we do and enjoy doing. We must start on the road to discipleship. This is my subject: "On the road to discipleship: Building the Millions More Movement."

In the word "disciple" is the word "discipline." One of the things absent today is our willingness to discipline ourselves. In the Book of James in the Bible, we read about how the tongue may be a little a member in the body, but how big a fire a small spark can produce. Can any man or woman tame the tongue? We love gossip, slander, talking on a level that does not feed the spirit of goodness; we love feeding each other garbage. The tongue is a small member, but it is a powerful rudder that can turn around big ships.

An undisciplined tongue breaks up families, organizations, churches, mosques, and synagogues; and brings movement to a halt. The road to discipleship is the road to discipline. "If any man would be my disciple," Jesus said, "he must first deny himself." If you deny yourself, you will come up against opposing forces. When you decide to discipline yourself, your old behaviors are no longer attractive. Then, you have moved to the next step: You have picked up your cross. So many people want the crown, but they are running from the cross.

So many people talk about Jesus and how he died for them, as though they do not have to die. It is easy for some people to talk about how Jesus paid the price on Cavalry, but when the time comes for them to pick up their cross, they believe their tithes are sufficient. Sometimes the church, mosque, and synagogue pay more attention to money than sufficing the needs of the people, so the people wonder if they are only present to give money.

Leaders and ministers look like pimps. Jesus said, "Whoever would be your minister"—not let him be your pimp—but "let him be your servant." If you make money the goal, rather than saving people, then you will lose both people and money. Jesus said, "I am going to make you a fisher of men."

Are ministers happy because your houses are full? Are you satisfied that you have fished enough, or have you stopped fishing because all the ministers' needs are met, so we do not care about the people who are swimming in the sea of filth and sin?

The whole objective of Jesus was not to build a church, mosque, or synagogue, but to build a community of people so that—not the walls are consecrated to God—but human beings will be a consecrated house, a temple with the indwelling spirit of the Living God, as it was when the prophets walked among us. We cover ourselves with a religious look, perfume ourselves with the odor of praise, and give to be seen of men and women, so that we can continue to indulge ourselves in wickedness yet maintain high visibility in the House of God. "If any man would be my disciple, pick up your cross."

After asking his disciples to deny themselves and pick up their crosses, Jesus told them, "Follow me." He did not tell them to worship him. The Bible says, "God is a spirit and those who worship Him must worship Him in spirit and in truth, for such the Father seeketh." Jesus never taught people to worship him.

Yet, you sit around praising Jesus and doing wrong; talking about Jesus and continuing your wicked ways. Jesus said, "If any man would be my disciple," not any "Black man" or "White man." So, the door to him is open to everybody who is willing to deny self, then you can come as you are, but you cannot stay as you are. He said, "Come and follow me."

t was difficult and demanding for people to walk behind Jesus in Rome. He was preaching about a kingdom, not preaching about democracy, or telling people to vote for the corrupt way of an empire or join the empire and fight for the corrupt power of Caesar. He was telling people to follow him because his kingdom is not of this world. We must understand that the discipleship and the Movement has to go hand in hand.

***

If you believe, from the Bible's view in the Chapter of Genesis, that God created the human being after His own image and likeness, how could we be the likeness of God physically and not the likeness of God spiritually? He created man and gave him dominion and power to rule the fowl of the air, the fish of the sea, and every creeping thing that crawls upon the earth, and gave him a command, "Multiply, replenish the earth, subdue it." Make the earth respond to the wisdom of God; take out of the earth what I, God, have put in it and make yourself a paradise on the earth.

But you are unable to do this because you have been following the wrong knowledge and lost your power. God forbade Adam from eating from the Tree of Knowledge of Good and Evil. Women do not talk to snakes. When a man wants to get to a woman, he romances her, gets close to the ear, and starts whispering and breathing in her ear. He breaks you down through the organ of the ear, but he is after something else. The ear is the means to get to the goal. Satan and God use the same thing. The Bible says, "Him that hath ears, let him hear," because life is going to come in a word, and light will be in that word, and if you would open your ears to the word, then God will come into you through your ear, like Satan comes in by tickling your ears.

God made Adam his khalifah, which means successor, or one who stands in the place of God and rules by His permission. How can man stand in the place of God yet not have the potential to reflect God? Women who ask where is their part in this process. In the fifth chapter of Genesis, it reads, "Male and female, created He them and called their name Adam." Men are not going anywhere without women, and we cannot do anything without women. Women are the natural partners of men, in righteousness and in crime.

When you listen to the wrong call or voice tickling your ear, you can be led astray. The first thing that Adam did that created death was rebelling against direct orders that came from God. The devil is wise because he knows how to come through the truth to make you deviate from the truth. After Adam rebelled and ate the Forbidden Fruit, his eyes came open to another world within himself. You have two worlds in you: one world revolves around your appetites and the other world revolves around an enlightened mind and spirit. These worlds are always struggling for supremacy.

Which world do you want to live in? Do you want to live in the world of an enlightened mind and spirit or the world of satisfaction of your appetites? The world of your appetites starts from the navel down; it is called the underworld, and it is ruled by Satan. So, you have to overthrow a foster father who you do not belong to; you have to overthrow the government, not in Washington, but in your head. If God is ruler in your dome, then your life reflects that God is present. You are not being what God created you to be; you are living in the underworld and Satan is the master of the underworld.

Scripture says, "As by one man sin entered into the world, and death came by sin," all men have sinned, so all men are dead, in terms of who they are and their capacity to be reflections of God. You are so far in reflecting God, but you reflect Satan, as liars, thieves, and murderers.

The Bible says they had the mark of the beast in their hands and foreheads. You are in a cemetery. The Bible says, "There is a way that seemeth right unto man but the ends thereof are the ways of death. The Holy Qur'an says that Satan makes evil fair-seeming. We are committing horrible acts, yet we think it is OK.

Although our bodies are flesh and comes from the earth, the Holy Qur'an says, "To God is my eventual return." But you cannot return from where you did not come. This body is the garment that clothes the spirit. The spirit comes from God. He is the Life-Giver. The spirit resides in the flesh, but how we use that energy is dependent upon who will steward our life.

Scriptures say train up the child in the way it should go, and when it is old, it will not depart from that. But you have not been stewarded by wise mothers who understood who they are. Instead, we have been under the stewardship of satanic, fallen man, fallen woman, fallen education, fallen system of jurisprudence, fallen society, and fallen religion.

Religion has failed to cultivate the human being and make them reflective of our Creator. Religion has touched you, because you are the people of God, you naturally feel that spirit, but you are not being encouraged to translate that energy into submission to the Will of God.

You are dead in the cemetery of your flesh. This body is the grave of your spirit. This is why Jesus taught the difference between a spiritual mind and carnal mind. When you are of the carnal mind, you are living for the satisfaction of the flesh. So, a trumpet has to sound. A trumpet only means a brassy truth that will touch you in your grave and quicken the Spirit of God that is already in you.

That spirit rising within you will cause you to be exorcised of the demons that now control you. Whenever the man of God appears that threatens Satan's world, Satan makes you think that he is a wicked and evil man, and you start hating a man who actually represents your rise from your grave.

The Honorable Elijah Muhammad was raised from the dead. He raised me, Malcolm X and Muhammad Ali. He raised us from our former condition and grew us into men who challenged a wicked government and system. We frightened people because God had put a new spirit in us, while the vast majority in the church, mosques, and synagogues are hypocrites. Nobody dares speak out against the wickedness within its own ranks.

My discipleship has allowed me to cast off self, denying the life I lived and the career. I had to become proficient in a word that would give life to my people. I first denied myself. When I came out of show business, making fairly good money, to find a job making hardly no money, my wife stood by my side.

Then I picked up my cross. I have been in this work for 50 years. They try to kill me and my whole family for a word that I teach. They call me everything that I am not for a word that I teach. I am rejected of men because what I teach upsets White folks. How can you be popular standing for God and righteousness in the midst of the wickedness that we see every day? I picked up my cross and I dared to follow him.

So, I am hated among men for his namesake. I know what it is like to be rejected. Who were the enemies of Jesus in ancient Rome and who are my enemies in this modern Rome? It was the scribes; it was the press. And the press today do not have any good things to say about Farrakhan.

God is angry. The Judgement of God has entered America like never before, so do you want to come correct? Do you want to be a better person? Do you want to come out of your grave?

11

Conspiracy and Betrayal

Nothing that the survivors of Hurricane Katrina have suffered was in vain because what they have suffered has brought our people together in a way that I have not seen in a long, long time. I heard gratitude in the voices of the victims—who were not just victims of Katrina because, while Katrina came from God, the flooding was man-made.

No matter what they lost—and they lost a lot—I heard praise of God, thanks to God for having spared their lives through the horror of their experience and bringing them through even though we lost many lives.

This is not a time for weakness or cowards. This is a time for strength. I say humbly that the sacrifice of life is necessary for the advancement of human beings towards the perfection of God.

There has been no advancement in science, medicine, technology, or engineering that has not been accompanied by the loss of life. There never has been a bridge built over a wide expanse that somebody did not die to produce that progress. There has never been a tunnel built underwater to connect two bodies of land that life was not lost to give human progress.

When I was a little boy, tuberculosis was a scourge among Black people. But the more people died from tuberculosis, the longing got stronger and stronger for a cure. So, it was death that produced a baby that would end the scourge, by discovering a cure. Out of the wombs of women come children who will answer the longings of people.

When we go to Mecca during hajj, there is a time for the slaughter of animals and every pilgrim has to sacrifice the life of an animal. Before the Kingdom of God can be established; before the scourge of White Supremacy and racism can end, and a government of peace, freedom, justice, and equality can be established, there must be a sacrifice of life.

The chicken that we eat wanted to live; but we are the superior life. So the lesser life is sacrificed for the greater life. All living things struggle to keep its life; but the supreme life is the human being, so the lesser life is sacrificed for the benefit of the supreme life. God is the Supreme of beings. So all of our lives are for a purpose bigger than our life.

Many people questioned how God could be present in such a tragedy. God is always present. Whether it is during a tragedy or a triumph, He is present. The tragedy in life is a trial for us. The triumph is also a trial. The tragedy of Louisiana, Mississippi and Alabama is a trial for the mayor, governor, president, his cabinet, FEMA, Red Cross, United Way, Salvation Army, B'nai B'rith, and all those who lost their lives and their possessions.

But it is also a trial for us because their suffering presents us with a question that we have to answer: How much do we love our people? How much of the love of Jesus Christ that we talk about is in our hearts? How much of the love of Prophet Muhammad (PBUH) that we talk about is in our hearts?

When we hear the cry and pain of our Brothers and Sisters, it is not enough to send money, clothes or food, because those are things that many of us can part from. What is required is to open our hearts and doors and let our family come in. They have given us a reason to live, organize and maximize our power and deal with the enemies that put them in this condition.

If we fail them in this hour, I will pray that Allah (God) will bring upon us the worst chastisement that He has ever brought upon a people in the annals of history. We will be worthy of death if we do not rise in this hour for the people of Louisiana, Mississippi, and Alabama. We must rise for all of our suffering people, but our focus should be on them. They have given us a cause. They have given the Millions More Movement a reason beyond the general reason why we were coming together. They gave the Movement specificity.

Katrina destroyed a lot of property with wind and rain, but while it was building up in the Gulf for a long time, FEMA and the government could have been ready. It did not just rush on New Orleans, Louisiana, and Mississippi all of a sudden. It was a Number 12 tropical storm when it touched Miami, the southern part of Florida. Then, it became a Category 1 hurricane.

What is the difference between a Number 12 tropical storm and a Category One hurricane? It is the degree of organization within a storm. As a storm increases its organization within itself, it progresses in category. When Hurricane Katrina grew into a Category 3 hurricane, it stayed awhile to give people a chance to move. When it became a Category 5 hurricane, its degree of organization was so great that it became the most powerful, destructive force, even that of megaton and atomic bombs.

The organization of Katrina made people leave what they did not want to leave. Its organizational power struck fear in people. This is why the number one denial objective of our enemy is that Black people must never be allowed to organize. We are so filled with fear, distrust, and envy that the enemy can control us because, either we are afraid to stand up like men and women; we distrust our leaders who will stand up for us; or we are envious because someone is doing something that we think we should.

Enemies are very close. I see too much hypocrisy in those who claim that they want a movement. Although they claim to be working with us, they are the agents of the enemy working to destroy a movement. But I warn you: I will call you out and sing a lullaby at your funeral. We have to examine the people who are up close around leadership, as Jesus was not betrayed from a distance. Some of our leaders do not want a movement.

While on my recent tour organizing for the Millions More Movement, members of the press asked me what happened to the movement, since I am saying some of the same things that I said 10 years ago when I was mobilizing for the Million Man March. It started great, but all of a sudden it petered out. They asked me how the Millions More Movement would be different.

I said the difference this time is what is written in the scriptures. You have heard all the teaching you are going to hear; you do not need any more teaching or preaching. You need a whipping, and it is on the way. We have been playing with God and marketing Jesus like a product, but no one is walking behind him. You think praising his name will get you into the Kingdom of God? But if you are not willing to walk the walk, then you should keep His Name out of your mouth, because you are nothing but a lying hypocrite.

You either are going to do or there will be a lot of death—not the few that we saw in Mississippi, Alabama, and Louisiana, but death is in the house now. The Wrath of Allah (God) has entered America and it is not going to stop. One calamity after another will hit America until America is laid low.

How dare you say that Black people are American citizens! When did we become citizens? We should stop talking foolishly. If we were citizens, we would have the rights of citizens. We have to accept reality. We are nothing but the same slaves that our great grandfathers were, and this country is a plantation. White citizens received help during the aftermath of Hurricane Katrina, while the Black so-called citizens were denied help by the government. There are sick-minded Negroes who want to be accepted by our former slave-masters and their children, rather than be accepted by God.

You are like the prodigal son depicted in the Bible, who left his father's house, squandered everything that he had at home and tried to join on to be a citizen in a strange land. He was given cheap jobs, husking corn, and feeding swine. When a famine came in the land, the prodigal son was down; after he remembered his father's house, he realized he was attracted to the strange land.

This is that strange land. You are attracted to this land because of the wealth of this land and the false promise that America is good for everyone. But you are nothing more than a mannequin in the window of democracy, wearing the garment of democracy to sell the lie to our people that this system works. It does not work for us and it never will work for us. It must be destroyed and something new and better brought in its place.

The prodigal son said he came to himself because he was other than himself—like you are. With all that you claim to know, you are not yourself. When he came to himself, he said, "I think" —he started thinking again—"I think I will arise and go to my family."

What is the Millions More Movement about? The Movement is a journey. The journey is not to make you a citizen. I don't want to integrate into this filth and abomination. Do you want democracy or the Kingdom of God? What are you praying for? Why do you recite the Lord's Prayer? "Thy Kingdom come, Thy will be done on earth..." That is not democracy; that is the Kingdom of God, and you are not going to get any joy or peace in this world.

Your joy and peace are in the Kingdom of God when it comes to the earth.

Then, all of humanity will never have to suffer like we have suffered and continue to suffer.

The flooding of New Orleans was a conspiracy. Hurricane Katrina was the cover for some dirt. The winds blew. The rains came on the Monday. By Tuesday, they were gone. People were standing in the French Quarter. There wasn't any water in the Ninth Ward after Katrina left. Then, the levee broke. How did it break? The homes that we saw in the Ninth Ward looked like they were intact, but water came all the way up to the top of the roof. The hurricane did not blow them away neither did the water come when Katrina came. The water came after Katrina left.

God is challenging us by this tragedy, to see if we will stand up for our people. When you stand up for them, you are standing up for yourselves. We are angry at what happened to our family, but today they know that they are loved. The brotherly love level among us, which was not there before Katrina, has increased—like there was no unity between the Democrats and Republicans on Sept. 10, 2001, but after Sept. 11, they found a reason to come together. Hurricane Katrina is our reason. We must channel our anger into a constructive energy to mobilize and build a movement.

There is a subtle undermining of the spirit to mobilize. On the surface, our leaders look good, but underneath there is rotten behavior and character. I was with Kathy Hughes recently at Radio One/TV1 and she asked me who were the co-conveners of the Millions More Movement. She looked at the list I handed her and said that there are four people on that list who have told her they have nothing to do with the Millions More Movement. I did not ask her who it was, but we simply have to deal with that kind of hypocrisy. Everybody does not want this Movement to be successful.

President George Bush is upset over the Millions More Movement. It is good that he's upset, but it is bad that he can get upset and make anointed people into his magicians. Pres. Bush acted irresponsibly and it was not until New Orleans Mayor Ray Nagin cursed him that he visited New Orleans after Hurricane Katrina hit. But why did he bring Bishop T.D. Jakes? He knew he had messed up with Black people and he knew Black people respected T.D. Jakes, so he wanted T.D. Jakes to clean him up in front of a people that he was negligent towards.

Mayor Nagin said there was a 25-foot crater under the levee. He did not say a bomb. I read that some of the scientists at LSU disagreed with the report by the Army Corp of Engineers that it was the water that topped the levee; the scientists at LSU said that did not happen. Later, they said, "We don't know what happened, but that did not happen."

Then, I received another bit of information from the Hal Turner Show, saying that a member of the Army Corp of Engineers saw burn marks on the concrete of the levee, took some of the concrete and spirited it away in his vest and sent it to his friends in the Armed Forensic Laboratory, and they found two different explosives that were used that citizens could get, for they were underwater explosives from the military. Maybe, this is a rumor, but residents of the Ninth Ward said that they heard explosions. The enemy was quick to say it was gas explosions in houses—but when the water came, they did nothing.

One of the evacuees who spoke, charged that it was a conspiracy. She is right. It is a conspiracy to drive the poor Blacks out of New Orleans. Why would they put the evacuees on a plane, without telling them where they are going? Then, they end up in Utah, California, or Colorado, only to be surrounded by armed guards?

In Georgia, the mayor of Macon visited me and told me that there were 600 evacuees in his city, but you cannot get to them without permission, and they cannot leave without permission. It is like they are in a detention camp. Some of the evacuees are even housed in discarded prisons.

The Millions More Movement has no validity unless the Movement uses the man-made and God-made tragedy as the centerpiece for the Millions More Movement. If reparations is our main focus, then these Brothers and Sisters, and the horror that they have been through, have to be healed—not just with money and homes. FEMA and the other charities are not culturally sensitive to the needs of our people or the psychological and emotional traumas that they have suffered.

So, on October 14 in Washington, D.C., at Howard University, 25 major Black organizations will be meeting, including Black doctors, nurses, psychologists, psychiatrists and sociologists, to prepare a plan to adopt families and put them under the type of care that they need to make them whole and wholesome.

In trying to make our Brothers and Sisters whole, we will become whole in the process. So let us organize a movement and let us turn our anger into a protest. Let us start moving toward Washington.

Let them know that we do not appreciate what the government has done, and then lay out before our people a plan of what we are going to do to challenge this government and heal our condition.

12

The Honorable Elijah Muhammad
And the Millions More Movement

Fresh off the road of traveling during his six-week intensive national tour of 23 cities, calling for the mobilizing and organizing of the Millions More Movement, Minister Farrakhan sat with Final Call *Managing Editor Dora Muhammad to discuss the Millions More Movement and its relationship to the work and words of the Most Honorable Elijah Muhammad.*

Final Call: What are your feelings today upon completing such an intensive and critical tour?

    Honorable Minister Louis Farrakhan (HMLF): Relief. I am thankful to Almighty God Allah that I could visit the number of cities in which I was blessed to travel. I never lost my voice in any city, yet I spoke sometimes from morning to night. I cannot judge the tour because I am the instrument that is being used, but the effect of the tour will be seen, by the Grace of God, on October 15. I felt great love from the people who attended the meetings and rallies.

    I was also encouraged and inspired by the level of scholarship of those to whom I spoke and their desire to help lift the masses and bridge the disconnection between the learned of our people and those who are not learned. I am filled with hope that we can link the learned to the masses in a programmatic way.

FC: On numerous occasions, you referred to an instruction from the Honorable Elijah Muhammad 32 years ago to you—serving then as the minister of the temple in New York—to bring the learned of that city to Chicago, so that they could help save the Nation. He delivered a lecture and then dismissed them. What do you recall of the lecture that the Honorable Elijah Muhammad gave to the learned at that time?

HMLF: I recall the fact that he told the learned that he had already planted and grew a tree and the fruit of that tree was good, it just needed manure to nurture it. He told them that we did not have to plant another tree, but should nurture the tree, and that there was enough fruit on the tree to feed us all. He also talked about the learned, that if they helped the unlearned, the unlearned would carry them on their shoulders and lift, admire, love and respect them for lifting them.

FC: Why did not the learned accept the program then?

HMLF: The Honorable Elijah Muhammad did not give them an opening to accept what he asked me to call them there for. It may not be that they did not accept the program, but he did not give them the opening to come in to help the Nation with the program—because he already knew that the Nation was going to fall. What he was actually doing was planting a seed that would come up 32 years later in the consciousness of his minister.

FC: Was there a specific event that triggered your recollection of that lecture?

HMLF: I cannot exactly recall, but I had no intention whatsoever of doing anything for the 10th Anniversary of the Million Man March. When people would ask me, I would answer no. Then eventually, I said, let me think about it. Somewhere in that period, my mind returned to 32 years ago to what he asked me to do then—and I knew that it was not for then, it was for now; for me to call the learned of our people and link them, through his program, to the lifting of the masses of our people.

FC: The Muslim Program—though called "Muslim"—is not only for Muslims. Can you explain the universality of the Muslim Program?

HMLF: If we look at those prophets whose teachings are to be universal, Jesus and Muhammad, we see that they started with a specific focus to a specific people whom God was going to use as an instrument to bring a message universally.

Jesus told his disciples, "Go not into the way of the Gentiles, and into any city of the Samaritans enter ye not, but go rather to the Lost Sheep of the House of Israel." That was a very limited and specific focus. Later, he told them, "Go ye into all the world and preach this gospel to every nation, kindred and tongue."

Though the message started with a limited focus, the germ of its universality was present, but the people whom God was going to use to spread that message universally had to be brought up to that point. So, it was with Prophet Muhammad of Arabia (Peace be upon him).

He started with a specific focus on the Arabs, and their great ignorance, disunity, and immorality. He focused on them with the revelation of the Holy Qur'an. While he was building them into a nation, he also appealed to the leaders of Rome and Persia. During his time among the Arabs, he reached beyond the Arabs, so that after his death, they would begin to move out universally. They went westward toward Africa, northward into Europe and eastward toward China.

So, they spread the message of Islam to the known world, at that time. The Honorable Elijah Muhammad started with a limited focus on the Black man and woman of America; then a broader focus to Black people wherever we are found on the earth; then, another broader focus to all of humanity.

That is suggested in the Muslim Program, which reads: "We want freedom. We want a full and complete freedom. We want justice. Equal justice under the law. We want justice applied equally to all regardless of creed or class or color." So, we have the universal approach, but it is a process of growth for us to grow up into the message; first seeing it as good for us, and then growing to see our mission, which is to bring this message on the universal plane to all the people of the earth.

FC: The root of the Muslim Program is the Honorable Elijah Muhammad, but throughout his work among us, his image and work have been sullied and slandered by the enemy. So cleaning up his image was a prerequisite for you doing your work among us. In the meetings with the learned and leadership during your tour, have you witnessed an acceptance of him or is there still a veil over him and they just see the wisdom?

HMLF: There is still a veil over him, but the more they accept his student—the student's job is to lift the veil off his source of guidance and inspiration. The scriptures say, "If I be lifted up from the earth, I will draw all men unto me." So, somebody has to do the lifting. The student is made attractive, by the Grace of God, to his people and many in other nations. The more attractive the student is, and he constantly reminds them that he is a student, then he is gradually lifting the veil off his teacher. Then, the people will see that he is backed by a power much, much, much, much bigger and greater than himself.

FC: Since they have been, and are, sullying your image, do we have to, in like manner, clean up your image in order to help you complete your assignment, and has our slowness been an impediment to you in completing your assignment?

HMLF: I do not blame the Believer because I have never tried to teach the Believer about myself scripturally. The Honorable Elijah Muhammad specifically told me not to worry about where I was in the scripture, but to make his great commission known and he would represent me to the people. So I go about doing my work.

Even though they have attempted and have sullied my image, the more Allah (God) blesses me with time and guidance to do the work that I am doing, the image is gradually cleaned—not because of them, but because of God guiding the Minister in a such a way that people see him clearer and know him better. Then, the glass that the enemy dirtied, God cleans it and the people see the Minister as he is, and then see the Messenger and the God as they are.

FC: What is our duty to you then, as your students?

HMLF: Your duty is to follow. If you take the example of the Minister, one of the main examples of the Minister is his humility. He does not think more of himself than he should, so he is not easily offended. He knows how to take much from the ignorance of the people, and he loves them more than they hate themselves. So he is gradually winning, not by fighting them, but giving them blessings for their cursings, and expressing his love for them in ways that ultimately overpower their dislike, hatred and envy of him.

The duty of the Believer is to follow that example for the benefit of the redemption of our people. The people will gradually see the followers; through the humility of the followers, the people will see the Minister; and through his humility, they will see the Messenger; and through the Messenger's humility, they will see God.

FC: What do you think the Honorable Elijah Muhammad thinks of the Millions More Movement?

HMLF: A Sister called me and told me of a dream where she saw the Honorable Elijah Muhammad. He was holding small meetings with select people. He said to her, "Tell the Minister that there is much that he sees and there is much that he does not see, but I see what he sees and I see all that he does not see. Tell him about this Millions More Movement, on that day, I will be completely in charge. Then, he said, I want to see him and my son Wallace, because I want my family to know that I am alive."

When she told me that, tears came from my eyes because I felt that I needed confirmation. Through that experience that she had, I received my confirmation. Right after that, Hurricane Katrina came, and after that you can tell that God, Himself, is involved in the creation of the Movement—which is the beginning of the making of a nation.

FC: The Honorable Elijah Muhammad said that, "Through you, he will get all of his people." How does that statement correlate to the Millions More Movement?

HMLF: It demonstrates that there is something that Allah (God) has put in the Minister that allows him to touch the hearts of people who are adversaries, friends or neutral because they do not know or understand. When you see people coming to the Minister, you know that whether he is living or dead, the things that God is inspiring him to say and do will reach people and bring them to the Honorable Elijah Muhammad.

FC: The Honorable Elijah Muhammad said words about the Christian preachers similar to what he said about the learned.

HMLF: The question was asked, "Will the Christian pastors accept Islam?" He answered in one word, "Yes." He said, when they come it will be a sign of the end, because these persons have traditionally been instruments of the slave-master. So, when he loses them as his instruments, they become the true instruments of God.

With their understanding of scripture, spirit, and anointing, they will take our people overnight spiritually and bring them up in the way of God.

FC: The enemy is working on the pastors, to some success, to separate the unity and love we have shared. How will we again bridge the gap of division?

HMLF: It is written in the Holy Qur'an that Pharaoh was afraid that the slaves would change their religion. Moses and Aaron were having an impact on the Children of Israel. So Pharaoh summoned the elders of Israel and promised them wealth and nearness to him, if they would oppose Moses and Aaron.

That was for a limited season. Then, the scriptures say that they finally submitted to the God of Aaron and Moses, and Pharaoh said, "How could you submit before I give you permission." So, they are going to submit. Right now, the government is afraid that the people are going to accept Islam, so they are summoning the pastors to oppose the Minister and create an impediment for the development of the Movement. But all of that is short-lived.

FC: While on tour, you stated that the disaster of Hurricane Katrina marked that the Judgement of Allah (God) had entered America, which will be your subject for the Commemoration of the 10th Anniversary of the Million Man March. You

also mentioned that this means, according to the scriptures, that God has sealed His elect in their foreheads. Who are the elect and what are they elected to do?

HMLF: Elect means that they are chosen. Scriptures say, "If it were not for His elect's sake, and those days be shortened, no life would be saved." So it is the chosen of God that He wants to bring through the Judgement that causes the shortening of the days of His Wrath.

Revelations, says, "Hold back the four winds, until I go down and seal my elect in their forehead, with the seal of the Living God." That seal is knowledge.

When a king writes a communication, he seals it, which says it is from him. So God sealing His elect in their foreheads with the seal of the Living God, means He is putting in their heads and hearts the stamp of His acceptance, approval, love and ownership of them. That is dangerous when you interfere with what God has put His seal on.

FC: When previous disasters have occurred, you have said that it is our righteousness that will allow us to survive the worst that is yet to come. What does this mean?

HMLF: When the death angel came through Egypt, the only thing that caused the death angel to pass over the houses was that the Children of Israel took the blood of the lamb and made a mark like an "X" on the doorpost of their homes. This represents the life of the Messenger, the life of Islam, the life of righteousness that will cause the death angel to pass over us.

The Honorable Elijah Muhammad actually said, "It is your righteousness that shall sustain you." That is a big difference from "survive." "Sustain you" means that you may go through something horrific but, through your righteousness, you shall be sustained in faith; you will not weaken. Your righteousness will give you the power to sustain and maintain your faith.

The Holy Qur'an warns, "Be careful of a chastisement that will not afflict those of you exclusively who are unjust." So it does not mean, when the chastisement comes, simply because we claim God and are trying to do right that it will not afflict us. The Holy Qur'an says, "When a misfortune befalls the Believer, the Believer says, "Allah is my Patron and to Him is my eventual return."

FC: Thank you for your time.

13

Unity Generates
Power To Change Reality

The most important thing that has happened today—which has never happened in our history—is that we have seen an unprecedented number of Black leaders of organizations coming together to speak to America and the world with one voice. Our whole spectrum of Black thought was represented here on the stage in front of the Capitol of the United States of America. This tells us that a new day is dawning in America and the world, starting with the unity of "the dry bones in the valley."

This is more than a moment in time, for no matter how many people who came, if there is a million or less or more, the meaning of this day is not today; the meaning of this day will be determined by what we do tomorrow to create a real movement among our people.

The time has never been more ripe for a strategic relationship between the Black, Brown, Native American and the poor of this nation and the world. Hurricane Katrina showed us the neglect of the United States of America, the failure of state government, federal government, and local government to answer the critical needs of our people.

I put more attention on the federal government, because there were four hurricanes last year that hit Florida and there was no neglect, or very little that we read of; certainly, there was no great loss of life. What happened to the federal government's response to the suffering victims of Hurricane Katrina and what lessons are we to learn from this? I believe that we can charge the government with criminal neglect of the people of Louisiana and Mississippi, and New Orleans in particular.

While we cannot sue the federal government, we can sue Homeland Security and FEMA for criminal neglect. We need to consider a class action lawsuit on behalf of the citizens of New Orleans who have lost everything because the government is not acting responsibly to give them back what they have lost and return them to their homes.

If a mother leaves her child in her car on a hot day to run into a supermarket, locks the door and windows, and stays a little longer than she had planned, and comes out to find her child is dead, certainly it was not her intention to kill her child. But the law says it was criminal neglect. For five days, the government did not act after Hurricane Katrina hit, and lives were lost. I cannot say what the intention was of the government; I will leave it to others to make that determination.

But I firmly believe that, if the people on those rooftops had blond hair, blue eyes and pale skin, something would have been done in a timelier manner. We charge America with criminal neglect. I hope that the lawyers will look into that, because a class action lawsuit on behalf of those who have suffered is absolutely necessary. We need to call witnesses to the witness stand under the oath of being able to be charged with perjury. We want to know what happened to the levee. We do not want to guess about it or be guilty of following rumors. We want to know what happened to that levee that caused the suffering of thousands of people.

Now, they are saying that they do not even want to rebuild the 9th Ward. So where will those residents live? The government will not do what they should do if we do not do what we must do. I understand that there are nearly 2,500 of our children missing. Nobody seems to know where they are. That is a crime of great proportions in a country where, I recently learned, 70,000 children from poor nations around the globe are here in sex slavery. Where are our children?

Can we stand by and allow it to be said that 2,500 of our babies are missing and we will not rise up, as a people, to demand to know where our children are? That is an ugly picture, Brothers and Sisters, and those kinds of pictures will continue until and unless we see the need to organize and mobilize.

On the 1st of September in Atlanta, Ga., a meeting of the elders took place that was inspired by a 5-year-old girl who was having a bad day in Florida, and we saw police put that little girl in handcuffs, shackle her feet and put her in the back of a police car. The police authority would not release that child to her mother. They are being sued today. Our grandparents, our parents, our youth, we have seen them all in chains. But now a new picture has evolved. We are seeing our babies in chains. Our people are being herded into the criminal justice system.

During the council of elders in Atlanta, Harry Belafonte, who is not only a great folk singer but also a marvelous and wonderful humanitarian, shared that one of his heroes is Eleanor Roosevelt. He said that Eleanor Roosevelt invited him to the White House along with Black leaders such as the distinguished A. Phillip Randolph. At the dinner table with President Franklin Delanor Roosevelt, A. Phillip Randolph stood to list a litany of abuses of Black people and a litany of things that President Roosevelt could do to ease those abuses.

Mr. Belafonte said that, when A. Phillip Randolph finished, the president did not speak immediately. He opened a box of cigars, passed cigars around to everyone at the table, and then said to A. Phillip Randolph, "Everything that you said about the abuses of your people I agree with and everything that you said I could do to end those abuses, I agree with. But Phillip, there's something that I want you to do." Mr. Randolph asked, "What is that, Mr. President?" and President Roosevelt said to A. Phillip Randolph, "Go and make me do it."

We should reflect on those words, as we stand on the Capitol steps and on this great Washington Mall. President Roosevelt may have been willing to do it, but he knew that if we did not organize enough force to make him do it, those around him would have stopped him from doing it.

As it was during the time of President Roosevelt, it has been throughout the presidencies, up to President George Bush today. The government will never do for the poor of this nation until and unless we organize effectively to make the government respond to the needs of the poor.

The burden is not on the White House; the burden is on us. Our 43 members of Congress, as brilliant and committed as they are, are impotent without the organization of those of us who need to see change. You would make a mistake and waste valuable time thinking that there is moral correctness in the government to serve the needs of the poor. That we must dispel. We must go back home and organize as never before. Hurricane Katrina grew to a Number 12 tropical storm and then she grew to become a Category 1 hurricane.

What was the difference between Katrina as a Number 12 tropical storm and a Category 1 hurricane? It was the degree of organization within that storm. The more organized it became, it went up in category, and then you saw people fleeing by the hundreds of thousands, fearing the consequence of the onslaught of a number 4 or number 5 hurricane. What is the lesson?

The more we are organized, the more we can generate power to change reality. The more we unify, the more power we can generate to change reality.

I thank Allah (God) for the leaders who spoke today, and I pray that we all are sincere, but I think that all of us in leadership need to be made accountable. There are those who are lip professors, who will come among us and say, "Surely, we are with you," as the Holy Qur'an says, "but when they are alone with their devils, they say, 'We are only mocking.'" But Allah (God) says in the Holy Qur'an, "In their hearts is a disease and Allah increases that disease because they lie."

All leaders must understand that this is a very dangerous time to play with the destiny of the people. If you love life, then do not play games with the destiny of a people who are crying to breathe free. Organizing is serious and there are those who do not want to see us unify.

This is written of in scripture, in the parable of a great image made of a head of gold, a breastplate of silver, legs of iron, and feet of iron mixed with miry clay. Gold is the heaviest metal; that is the head, so it is top heavy. That is the rich. The breastplate of silver represents the next richest. But the legs that support the head of gold have feet that have iron mixed with miry clay.

The Honorable Elijah Muhammad taught us that those feet represented the weakness of the world that we are living in. We are living in a world where the rich are a few and the poor are many, but it is the poor who are supporting the rich. That is why the rich hate anyone who can stimulate the consciousness of the poor. Those of you who are Christian, it was the poor who heard the message of Jesus gladly. The Roman rulers were frightened of Jesus, and they had to come against him, because stirring the poor is like troubling those feet of iron mixed with miry clay, since it was a weak foundation for such a heavy head. If you disturb the poor, the rich come down. So, a movement is dangerous to the few who have power over many.

Are you sure that you want a movement? Are you sure that you want to organize effectively to change your reality? If you are sure, then you should be ready for severe opposition. There is no idea worth anything that is not tested by opposition. Opposition is as necessary as the wind that blows and the sun that shines. In order to test the strength of the idea and the commitment of those who support the idea, we must be tested by opposition.

So, when we go back home, we should know that our work has just begun. What should we do when we go back home? Since the government has shown us that they really do not care, we cannot let another catastrophe come and we are not prepared.

The Bible says, "In the beginning was the Word, the Word was with God, the Word was God," but the Word did not stay a Word. The Word became flesh and dwelled among men. It makes no difference what we say, because a lot of us are good talkers. It will make a difference what we do. What we say can only become flesh if we go from this place and mobilize and organize, street by street, block by block, house by house so that we can accomplish that which we desire for the good of ourselves and our people.

We should form a Ministry of Health and Human Service. Jesus said, "Those who would be chief among you, let him be your servant." We, in leadership, and our organizations are not here to master the people, but to serve the people. So, if such a disaster comes again, we need a Ministry of Health and Human Service to look after the health needs of the Black, Brown, Native American and the poor.

President Fidel Castro, in Cuba, offered America over 1,500 doctors that spoke English to help with the tragedy of Hurricane Katrina. Our government, out of pride, did not accept those doctors. I think we should find a way to accept those doctors, because our people need medical attention. If the government will not permit us to do that, we have a just cause to make them show why we—who have hospitals closing in Washington and in cities across the country—do not need doctors.

President Castro has offered Blacks in America 500 scholarships to go to Cuba to study medicine with only one stipulation—that we must practice medicine in our own communities. Let us accept Fidel Castro's offer, and when our doctors return home, let us form a Ministry of Health and Human Service that we can use to serve the needs of the Black, Brown, Red and the poor of this nation.

We need a Ministry of Agriculture. The Black farmers are suffering. We need to unite our Black farmers, make their land productive and tie that land to the needs of the city. The Native Americans have the largest tracts of land and, according to what I learned from Brother Bob Brown of the All African Peoples' Revolutionary Party, they are willing to lease millions of acres if we are ready to go to work.

As long as we keep our mouths in the kitchen of our enemy, we will never have good health. We must provide food for ourselves because the merchants of death are feeding the American people and they are tied to the pharmaceutical companies. They create disease, on one hand, through the improper raising of food and livestock and then they make pills, on the other hand, to correct what they have created.

We need a Ministry of Agriculture, because farming is the engine of every nation and we need to provide for ourselves the things that we consume. This will cause us to want to build supermarkets in every city, canning factories, and frozen food factories so we can take our products from the ground, can it or freeze it, and put it into our own supermarkets.

We need a Ministry of Education. Let us unite all of our educators because the western system of education has run its course and is no longer worthy to hold our children or America's children. We are calling on our educators to provide a new educational paradigm. If our educators form themselves into a ministry, a service, then we will be able to educate our children and others and make a productive people.

We need a Ministry of Defense. Our young men are born soldiers, but they are in the wrong war. They are fighting a war in the streets of America against each other, or they are fighting an unjust war overseas in Afghanistan and Iraq. We need to bring our boys home and put them into the Ministry of Defense, so we can defend our communities, rather than destroy our communities.

We need a Ministry of Art and Culture. We applaud the hip hop community, the leaders of young people all over the world, but I want the young generation of artists to know there is a bigger purpose for art and culture than popping our fingers and shaking our backsides.

Mao Tse Tung, throughout his long march to conquer China, had a billion people whose lives he had to transform. Many of them were victims of opium, drugs, and prostitution, like we are. But Mao Tse Tung went to the cultural community, and they accepted his idea.

Then, through song, dance, poetry, drama, documentaries, movies and books, the idea of Mao Tse Tung became the idea of a billion people. China became a world power on the base of culture and the artistic community. If we had a Ministry of Art and Culture in every city, as we create this movement, we could say to our young people, "What is the idea of the Time and are you reflecting that idea in your songs, dance, and music?

We need a Ministry of Trade and Commerce. Do you think that a Millions More Movement should not be involved in the development of Africa, the Caribbean and Central America? If we started feeding ourselves, the billions that we spend on food could be spent elsewhere. We need clothing and shelter. Our clothes and shoes are made in another country.

If we pooled some of the money that we spend foolishly, we could set up factories in Africa and the Caribbean, where the labor market is a little cheaper than the labor here. If they made our clothes, then we could open up clothing stores all over America, sell them cheaper than the market and then capture the market of the people. Africa can be a source of shoes and clothing and lots of other things that we may not be able to successfully make in America. So, we need a Ministry of Trade and Commerce that can link the struggle here with Africa and the Caribbean, Central and South America. We have a market of nearly 90 million Black and Brown people. That is a huge market. We should tap that market so we will not have to beg others; we will be able to do it ourselves.

We need a Ministry of Justice. We need to look at the conflicts in our own community. We do not need to go to our slave-masters to solve our problems. We need to have a Ministry of Justice in every city that can solve the conflicts among us. We need a Ministry of Information. We need to gather all the Black newspapers and magazines, Black radio, and television stations into a Ministry of Information. If we have enough money in our ministry, we can send our reporters wherever we want to investigate the truth. We do not wish to be subjected to the Associated Press, Reuters, UPI or to the managed news of America and the world. We need to be where the action is so that our people will get correct information.

We need a Ministry of Science and Technology, and lastly, we need a ministry that deals with the head and spirit of our people. We need to collect our spiritual leaders of Christianity, Islam, Judaism, and other religions and develop a spiritual teaching that will transform our lives by renewing our minds, that we may destroy the Willie Lynch syndrome in Black people in America and throughout the world forever.

This assembly today is about the repair of ourselves and our people in Africa, the Caribbean, Central and South America. Allah (God) has given us the medicine to heal our condition. The government cannot heal us because they do not have any power to heal themselves. The medicine is with us to transform our lives. There is money in our community. We get a quarter of a trillion dollars into our hands. The education is among us. All we need is the will and the unity and we can repair what has been broken.

Dr. Conrad Worrill read a word from Brother Malcolm on reparations. That demand must be made, but it must be backed by the power of an organized people. Native Americans have demands to make of this government for lands and wealth that is due them, promises that were made, treaties that were broken, but they, of themselves, are weak to get what the government owes them. But together, we, as a united people, can make a demand on behalf of the Native Americans, ourselves, as well as the Latinos whose families are being broken up. United, we can solve these problems, but divided we keep injustice in power.

What are you fighting for in America's wars? You do not need to be in Iraq and Afghanistan. We need to be cleaning up the neighborhood where we live and stop the bloodletting where we live, and we can stop the White police from shooting us down. We demand that America do justice by the children of slaves.

We have not given up our place in Africa or our rights to Africa. Africa is ours and we should claim it and help rebuild it and make it the great power that Africa is destined to become. Brothers and Sisters of the Caribbean, Africa is trying to unite to form the United States of Africa. The Caribbean cannot continue to exist as little island nations. There must be a union of all the islands into a Caribbean Union with Venezuela and Cuba.

If those islands would unite, examine the value of their land to produce what they consume and then export their surplus, their unity will make the islands less marginalized in the future. The sugar cane industry and banana industry are gone. Why are we sending our children to colleges in the Caribbean? So that they can serve rich Black, White, and Brown people who come to lay up in the sun on vacation? We do not want to be the servants of others if we are not going to be the servants of ourselves. Unite Caribbean, unite.

The pace of the development of the United States of Africa is moving too slow. We want to help give you a little push because you are holding up the future of Africa's children by your slowness. Whatever we can do to help, we are your Brothers. We stand by you.

We are told in the Preamble of the Constitution that, if the government fails to give the people life, liberty, and the pursuit of happiness, we have the right to change the government. We have the right to reform it or abolish it. You have to decide, America, what you want to do. If you want to reform it, regime change is necessary, but you have to get out of power the neo-conservative idea of an imperialist America. We should take America back from the rich and give it to the people if it really is for the people.

To the union leaders who spoke today, you need to think over your pride because this government is destroying unions. It is destroying workers and the wages that workers and unions have fought to give the worker. So what should the worker do? Look at the billions that you have in pension funds? We should sit down together to examine the money and resources that we have collectively, and then start buying America. America is for sale.

We can buy tens of thousands of acres of land and begin food production, preparing warehouses and begin agribusiness. Labor leaders should get involved in producing a new food base and the billions that we spend on food will give jobs to the jobless and put money in the hands of the labor unions—but if the labor unions will not do it, let our unity do it. Let us put our finance together and build the Millions More Movement.

14

The Birth of A Nation

I want to say, first, how much I love you all and how grateful I am to Almighty God Allah to have a message in my mouth from the Honorable Elijah Muhammad that is destined to free us, as a people, and make us into a people that will be the cornerstone of the Kingdom of God.

Beloved pastors, my dear Christian family, I am so honored that you would honor us with your presence. We are your family and you are our family, and we will never let what is going on in the East drive a wedge between us in the West. We must be an example of how Muslims and Christians can live together in peace and brotherly love to accomplish the liberation of our people.

To my Christian family, whom I love dearly and deeply and will give my life for your liberation, as well as the liberation of our people, I cannot hesitate to say to you that it is an honor to live for you and it is even a greater honor to die in the cause of the liberation of our people.

When you fight for the liberation of your people, there is no death for you. There is only the death of the flesh; but when you give your life for a noble cause, as long as that cause endures, your life is in that cause.

***

One hundred and twenty-nine years ago today, February 26, 1877, a Man was born in the Holy City of Mecca in Arabia. He was born to a White mother and a Black father that He might have the right complexion to come among us without observation to do a job that was written of Him that He would search the earth for that people that was lost, and He would find them and bring them again and settle them on the mountains of Israel. That people that was lost is you and me, the Black people of Africa that were brought out of Africa on a westerly course to a north country and brought into slavery.

We were robbed, blind, deaf, and dumb. We have eyes, but we cannot see. We have ears, but we cannot hear. We have tongues, but we cannot speak. We have been classified by Allah (God) through the mouth of His prophets as mentally dead in the grave of ignorance and we must be resurrected from that grave.

In the Masonic order, there were those who tried to raise Hiram that did not have the right grip, so he slipped back into that shallow grave. But One came with the Master Grip. It was the Master. With the lion's paw, He reached down to pull Hiram out of the grave.

There is a lion asleep in Judah, but who is qualified to wake him? You are that sleeping lion, but Allah (God) has come to raise you out of your grave, as it reads in the 37th Chapter of Ezekiel, where it describes the dry bones in the valley. God says: "And when I have raised you out of your grave, then shall you know that I, the Lord, am God and beside me there is no Saviour."

When you look at the condition of Black people lost in America deep down in the muck and mire of a decadent civilization, we may wonder what power can raise the Black man from the condition that his ever-present tormentors have put him in. Only the power of God, the Power of a mighty Saviour, the power of the Son of Man can raise us. The scriptures say, "As lightning shineth from the East even unto the West, so shall the Coming of the Son of Man be."

The scriptures also says, "For wheresoever the carcass is, there shall the eagles be gathered together." You and I are the carcass of a once great people and mighty nation; and the symbol of America is an eagle, and that eagle has plucked the flesh of the carcass of our people.

But the Son of Man has appeared. The Son of Man has come. Why is he called the Son of Man? Because He is a man from a man, but He is also a Man Who is anointed with the wisdom and the power of God to deliver a nation of people from the hands of their oppressor.

One hundred and twenty-nine years ago, a man was born. He spent three-and-one-half years among us. He fulfilled the scriptures where it reads, "As Jonah was in the belly of the whale three days and three nights, so shall the Son of Man be in the heart of the earth." America is the heart of the earth and the heart of America is the Motor City, Detroit; and it was in that city that Master Fard Muhammad made His Appearance and it was in that city that He found a man named Elijah Poole, whom He gave the name "Muhammad."

I met that man, Elijah Muhammad. I was never blessed to see his Teacher, Master Fard Muhammad, but I love him, as my Hebrew Israelite family says, "with a perfect love." I love him because He befriended us when we had no friends. We cried out looking to a mystery God to do for us what no man has ever done for us and we tried that mystery God, and nothing happened until the Son of Man came.

One Father's Day, I was with the Honorable Elijah Muhammad. I was preaching on the beauty of the magnificent Lord's Prayer that Jesus gave to his disciples and I was comparing it to the oft-repeated prayer of the Muslims, the opening chapter of the Holy Qur'an, called *Al Fatihah* or "The Opening" or "The Key," because without the right kind of prayer in the right manner to the right source, you do not have the key to open up the Book of Wisdom or the secrets of life itself.

As I shared those thoughts with him, he said, "Brother, when I am gone, you can sit as the father of the house." "As" means that it is not your house nor are you the father. So, I thought that today I would speak to you as a father who loves the children of God in the House and wants to leave them with guidance and wisdom so that that guidance and wisdom may guide them when they may not see the father anymore or at least for a while. I love you as a father, but a father is a disciplinarian. A father who loves the child speaks straight words.

The Honorable Elijah Muhammad said, "I am a very rich man because Allah has given to me a Nation." So, I am not speaking as a father over a house of just Muslims—and yet, I am speaking as a father over a house of Muslims because Master Fard Muhammad said all of our people are Muslims. A Muslim is only one who submits his or her will to do the Will of God. You are the people of God, and your nature is to bow down to the Will of Allah (God).

Our problem is that we have not fully known Allah's (God's) Will. We are in the house of an alien or enemy of His Will that has taught, shaped, and molded us in rebellion against God. So even though we praise God with our lips, our hearts are far removed from Him, not because we want to be removed from Him, but our ignorance does not allow us to know His Will clear enough that we may do that Will.

Dear beloved pastors, our preaching today will be empty and void if we do not teach the people and show the people how the prophesies relate to the daily news. The daily news is not new. The prophets saw it and the prophets wrote it. There is so much good and truth in the Bible and we may study portions of it and teach it in a wonderful sermon. But unless it is related to the prophesies that talk about the time that we are living in, which is the end of a present world and its systems, then our preaching is not preparing the people to get through the end of a world.

***

Preachers and ministers are afraid to teach that Allah (God) is against certain activities and tell their congregations that they must clean up their lives of these activities. We are more concerned about the money that is given in the collection plate than raising people out of the satanic mind and spirit that the enemy is creating for us to live in and under. Woe unto that kind of preacher. That kind of preacher and teacher is condemned by Allah (God) and will eventually be condemned by the people.

As Allah (God) awakens the people, they will kill leaders and preachers in their pulpits for lying to them, deceiving them, and failing to study the Word of God and deliver the Word as it ought to be delivered—for the salvation of the people and not for entertainment.

The Bible says that the Judgement of God will begin first in the House of God. This fact should cause us to be nervous. If Allah's (God's) Judgement begins in the House, then the worse hypocrites are in religion. They talk God, but they live Satan—or should I say "we." I do not want to exclude myself, because I have to be judged along with everyone else.

Therefore, I am trying today to say what needs to be said, so that you will never charge me before God that I did not tell you and you will not be able to say, "I did not know."

Homosexuality, lesbianism, and transgender life has not been approved, and is not approved by the God of the Torah or the Old Testament, the God of the *Injil* or the New Testament, or the God of the Holy Qur'an. Even though we have to preach what Allah (God) says, we do not preach it out of hate, because none of us are so righteous that we can condemn another person who has adopted a pattern of life that is different from ours. Yet, I must tell you that Allah (God) does not approve of that way of life.

But in a country that says it is a democracy, every homosexual, lesbian and transgender person has the right to move in a society without fear of people beating, brutalizing, or killing them because of the way they are and live their life.

But I must tell you that Allah (God) has something in mind for all of us, to reform us, and make us into a people that will be a light to the world.

Appendix I

Thank You Letter

from Minister Farrakhan

IN THE NAME OF ALLAH, THE BENEFICENT, THE MERCIFUL.

October 19, 2005

As-Salaam Alaikum. (Peace Be Unto You)

To All Supporters and Participants of the Millions More Movement:

I am writing this letter to personally thank Reverend Willie Wilson (the National Director of the Millions More Movement), the National Executive Committee and all of the National Co-Conveners for their work to help create the Millions More Movement and to make the 10th Anniversary Commemoration of the Million Man March successful.

I would also like to personally thank all of the members of the Local Organizing Committees, the laborers and members of the Nation of Islam, members of Union Temple Baptist Church, and the many individuals and organizations for the great work that they did toward the success of the Mass Assembly on October 15.

My deepest apologizes to Mother Tynnetta Muhammad, india.arie and all of the musicians and dancers who worked so hard on behalf of her musical production; to Pam Africa and Mumia Abu Jamal, who sent a message from his prison cell to be read, to Ture Muhammad, George Fraser, Reverend Wendell Anthony, Reverend Albert Sampson, Reverend Herbert Daughtry, and to anyone who may have been omitted from the program.

The success of that day cannot be measured by what happened or did not happen, but the success of that day will be determined by how well we work to create a movement for the betterment of our people that will, Allah (God) willing, outlive us all.

I sincerely thank everyone for their good thoughts, their good desires and their good deeds toward the Millions More Movement.

I Am Your Brother and Servant,

signed

The Honorable Minister Louis Farrakhan
Servant to the Lost-Found
Nation of Islam in the West
HMLF/sm

Appendix II

Step by Step: Minister Farrakhan's MMM Tour

1
August 14
Milwaukee, Wisconsin

2
August 16
Detroit, Michigan

3
August 18
Indianapolis, Indiana

4
August 20
Chicago, Illinois

5
August 22
Cleveland, Ohio

6
August 24
Boston, Massachusetts

7
August 27
Brooklyn, New York

8
August 28
Mt. Vernon, New York

9
August 29
Newark, New Jersey

10
August 30
Waynesburg, Pennsylvania
Meeting with
Mumia Abu-Jamal

11
August 31
Philadelphia, Pennsylvania

12
September 1
Atlanta, Georgia
Council of Elders

13
September 2
Baltimore, Maryland

14
September 4
Richmond, Virginia

15
September 5
Washington, D.C.
Howard University

16
September 7
Norfolk, Virginia

17
September 9
Durham, North Carolina

18
September 10
Greensboro, North Carolina

September 11
Hurricane Katrina
Fact-Finding Mission
19 Dallas, Texas
20 Houston, Texas
21 Baton Rouge, La.
22 Jackson, Mississippi

23
September 12
Charlotte, North Carolina

24
September 13
Columbia, South Carolina

25
September 15
Atlanta, Georgia

26
September 17
Chicago, Illinois
Challenging the Genius

Educational Conference

27
September 19
Houston, Texas

28
September 21
Dallas, Texas

29
September 23
Memphis, Tennessee

30
September 24
Washington, D.C.
Congressional Black Caucus
Clergy Meeting

31
September 25
St. Louis, Missouri

32
September 27
Chicago, Illinois
Hurricane Katrina
Town Hall Meeting

West Coast Tour
Sept. 30 - Oct. 9
33 San Francisco, California
34 Los Angeles, California
35 Phoenix, Arizona

Appendix III

The Nine Ministries of the Millions More Movement

1 Ministry of Health and Human Service

2 Ministry of Agriculture

3 Ministry of Education

4 Ministry of Defense

5 Ministry of Art and Culture

6 Ministry of Trade and Commerce

7 Ministry of Justice

8 Ministry of Information

9 Ministry of Science and Technology

The Issues of The Millions More Movement

1. Unity. We call, first, for the unity amongst Black peoples and organizations. We call for unity amongst all African peoples and peoples of African descent worldwide. We call for unity with our Brown, Red, disenfranchised, and oppressed Brothers and Sisters in America, Caribbean, Central and South America, Asia, and all over the world. "The Power of One" is the synthesis of men, women, youth, and elders working in unity for our total liberation.

2. Spiritual Values. We call for Atonement, Reconciliation and Responsibility. We organize in the name of our God (The One Creator) and on sound ethical, moral principles and values. Our Movement affirms the rich legacy and diversity of our spiritual traditions and calls for unity and understanding among our religious faiths and spiritual traditions.

3. Education. We demand an end to substandard education in our community. The Millions More Movement advocates, and will develop, a new, independent educational paradigm for our people. We must have a knowledge of self, our history, and the best education in civilized society. We will build a skills bank, the talent of which will be used in the development of our people.

4. Economic Development. We will establish a Black Economic Development Fund, with the support of millions, to aid in building an economic infrastructure. We will also offer housing ownership opportunities to check the adverse tide of gentrification. The Millions More Movement will produce and distribute its own products and supports "Buy Black" campaigns.

5. Political Power. The Millions More Movement is the political voice of the poor and disenfranchised. We are resolved to take an independent political path in order to achieve political power. The Millions More Movement will be an organized political force of consequence in America and all over the world.

6. Reparations. We demand full and complete Reparations for the descendants of slaves. We demand that America take the appropriate steps to help in the repair of the damage done from 300 years of slavery, 100 years of segregation, and 50 years of the misuse and abuse of governmental power to destroy Black organizations and leaders.

7. Prison Industrial Complex. We demand freedom for all political prisoners held in U.S. prisons and detention facilities, both foreign and domestic. We demand an end to police brutality, mob attacks, racial profiling, the herding of our young men and women into prisons and the biological and chemical warfare perpetrated against our people.

8. Health. We demand an end to the lack of adequate health care in our community and we demand free health care for the descendants of slaves in this nation. The Millions More Movement will present a Preventive Health Care Plan to our people that will begin with a campaign to educate our people on healthy dietary, eating and exercise habits.

9. Artistic/ Cultural Development. We demand a greater accountability and responsibility of our artists, entertainers, industry personnel and executives, for them to commit to the redevelopment and upliftment of our people. We demand an end to the exploitation of our talent by outside forces. We will make strides in obtaining greater control over the means of production and distribution of our immense artistic talent and creative genius. We advocate for cultural development, and for the knowledge of our original culture to be used as a model for future advancement.

10. Peace. We call for the establishment of peace in the world. We demand an end to wars of foreign aggression waged by the United States Government against other sovereign nations and peoples. We demand an end to senseless violence, and advocate peace amongst street organizations (gangs) and youth.

ABOUT THE FINAL CALL FOUNDATION

Final Call Foundation

The Final Call Foundation was established in 2021 with the purpose to support raising awareness, preserving, researching, and amplifying the public works and personal history of the Honorable Minister Louis Farrakhan in the uplift of all humanity.

Follow us: 📘📷 @finalcallfoundation 🐦 @FCFcharity
Visit The Final Call Foundation Amazon Author Page for release updates

Available Titles

Sarah: Five Notes on a Woman's Prayer over Her Pregnancy

A Demonstration of Love *A special collection of articles and editorials*

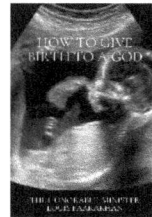

How To Give Birth To A God by the Honorable Minister Louis Farrakhan

Upcoming Titles

7 More Speeches by the Honorable Minister Louis Farrakhan

On the Sacredness of The Female

A Saviour is Born for the Black Man and Woman of America by the Honorable Minister Louis Farrakhan

ABOUT THE EDITOR

Dora Muhammad is an artist, author, and advocate. She served as editor-in-chief of *The Final Call* Newspaper from 2003-2006. In 2010, she founded The AWARE Project, a multimedia vehicle for advocacy on issues relative to women's awareness, engagement, rights, empowerment, and advancement. In 2018, she developed the heath equity program at the Virginia Interfaith Center for Public Policy, which she still spearheads along with her role as the center's Engagement Director. She earned a Bachelor of Arts in Journalism and Documentary Photography, with a concentration in Magazine Production and completed her photography thesis at Dartington School of the Arts in Devon, England. She worked as an arts administrator for Autograph-ABP (Association of Black Photographers) while studying International Law and Human Rights at the University of London. Dora earned her Master of Public Administration and has extensive work in government relations and public policy formation. A daughter of Indo-Caribbean immigrant parents, Dora is a native New Yorker who resides in Northern Virginia. She currently serves as the executive director of The Final Call Foundation.

Visit the Dora Muhammad and AWARE Project Amazon Author Pages for more information and updates on the catalog of her books.

www.ingramcontent.com/pod-product-compliance
Lightning Source LLC
Chambersburg PA
CBHW081401270326
41930CBC0015B/3372